RUSTIC
wrappings

Exploring Patina in Wire,
Metal, and Glass Jewelry

KERRY BOGERT

INTERWEAVE
interweave.com

To My Husband, To My Parents,
and To My Sister . . .
You make so much possible.

EDITOR: Erica Smith

TECH EDITOR AND ILLUSTRATOR: Bonnie Brooks

ART DIRECTOR: Liz Quan

DESIGNER: Karla Baker

PHOTOGRAPHERS: Joe Coca and Jack Deutsch

PHOTO STYLING: Ann Swanson

PRODUCTION: Katherine Jackson

Interweave Press LLC
201 East Fourth Street
Loveland, CO 80537
interweave.com

Printed in China by C&C Offset.

Library of Congress Cataloging-in-Publication Data
Bogert, Kerry.
 Rustic wrappings : exploring patina in wire, metal, and glass jewelry / Kerry Bogert.
    pages cm
 Includes bibliographical references and index.
 ISBN 978-1-59668-549-9 (pbk.)
 1. Jewelry making. 2. Wire craft. 3. Glass beads. I. Title.
 TT212.B639 2009
 745.594'2--dc23
                      2012002085

10 9 8 7 6 5 4 3 2 1

Contents

Introduction 4

Tools to Tinker with 6

Managing Metals 10

Basic Techniques 14

Patina Recipes and Sealing Solutions   26

Wire Embroidery 33

Exploring Rustic Color 36

Among Anemone Earrings   38
Blooming Twine Earrings   41
Analog Bracelet   44
Aurora Necklace   47
Candy Chandelier Earrings   50
Sprockets In Pockets Bracelet   53
Chrysanthemum Bracelet   56
Moroccan Archways Necklace   61
Mountain Bride Necklace   65
Seahorse Tales Earrings   70
Hidden Grace Bracelet   72
Tender Nest Necklace   76
Luna Unearthed Earrings   82
Wonder While You Wander Bracelet 85
Safe Passage Bracelet   88
Lilacs & Peonies Bangles   92
Creek Hill Necklace   96
Lazy Daisy Necklace   98
Spice Traders Earrings   103
Swiftly Bound Necklace   106
Wash Away Lariat   110
Just Because Earrings   114
The Mariner Necklace   116
Modern Plaiting Bracelet   119
Western Ways Bracelet   122

Meet the Bead Artists 125

Resources 126

Index 128

Carefree and fanciful; organic and natural; timeless and possible; passionate and sensible— evoking a romantic rendezvous set against a backdrop of a western sunset . . .

These are just a few of the images and emotions I hope you'll experience as you flip through the pages of this book. Isn't it amazing how jewelry can sum up a multitude of ideas all at once? Being able to express yourself in such a way can be a really powerful thing. Throughout my creative career, I have had the opportunity to explore several modes of self-expression. I sew, I knit, I paint, and I write. I always, always, find myself coming back to jewelry as my favorite means of communicating what is in my heart. As I bend, twist, hammer, snip, and otherwise manipulate wire, I capture in a necklace, bracelet, or earrings things that can sometimes be hard to say with words. It allows me to share with the world who I am and what I hope to be.

Most of the time, my jewelry uses bright and bold colors and shiny silver to evoke feelings of joy, fun, play, and youthfulness. However, in this book we will be exploring a more settled, earthly, organic, and wistful style of design that takes inspiration from life, love, nature and the elements, times gone by, and the hope of things to come.

One of the ways to create this thoughtful mood is to play with color. Copper roofs have amazing color, for example. So do old bronze sculptures. How could that be re-created on the surface of jewelry without leaving it in the rain for 100 years? How do you create rustic jewelry using methods that go beyond simply oxidizing, incorporating a wide variety of colors?

It's not as hard as you may think. I can't tell you how completely amazed I was the day I discovered that I could spritz a little salt water on metal floating in the fumes of ammonia to get a prettiest blue patina I had ever seen. I have to thank Linda and Opie O'Brien's *Metal Craft Discovery Workshop* (North Light Books, 2005) for introducing me to many of the patina methods I explore in this book. I used their techniques as a springboard into my own methods that I'll be sharing with you. I know you are going to love being a studio color scientist as much as I do!

As always, in these pages you will find not only the basics of jewelry making, but careful step-by-step guidance in how to work new techniques. This book also offers color tips and insights with you to kick-start palettes. I have had many conversations with students who tell me they fear color and often find themselves in a color rut. Fear is the last emotion that we would want to evoke in a jewelry design, so prepare to be inspired!

I can't wait to get started! So grab your pliers and let's get twisting . . .

– Kerry

TOOLS TO *tinker* WITH

One of the wonderful things about working with wire is that so many designs can be created using just three simple tools: round-nose pliers, chain-nose pliers, and wire cutters. As your skills grow and your ideas expand, so will your collection of tools. Don't be surprised if one day you catch yourself spying the utility hammer in the garage and wondering about the type of texture it would leave on the surface of flattened wire. (Been there, done that!) When you add sheet metal to your designs, and go so far as to add embroidery and patina to that metal as well, there are a few more things you'll need handy.

BASIC TOOLS

You don't have to spend a lot of money on pliers in order to create quality jewelry. The most important thing is that the pliers feel comfortable in your hand and that they get the job done. One item that is worthy of a larger investment is a set of wire cutters. There is nothing like a set of cutters that snips wire so cleanly that it doesn't need to be filed down.

Rosary or Round-nose Pliers

I prefer rosary pliers to traditional round-nose pliers. The shorter jaw length gives you more torque, or power, when bending heavy-gauge wire, but it can still make loops in a variety of sizes. They also have cutters below the jaws that work for quick rough cuts.

Chain-nose Pliers

My favorite grabbing pliers. I suggest you get two! I prefer these to flat-nose pliers because the narrow tip allows you to get into smaller spaces.

Flush Cutters

Flat on the back, V-shaped on the top. I strongly recommend investing in a higher quality brand of this tool. The nicer the cutter, the less filing down will be needed after the cut! (And don't ever cut memory wire with your flush cutters; it just isn't a pretty picture. Your cutting blades will become dented and unusable.)

Big "Daddy" Cutter

Larger, heavier cutters for snipping thicker gauges of wire. I use this most often when cutting 14-gauge and 16-gauge wire.

Bench Block

For hammering and work-hardening projects. I like the basic 2-by-2-inch (5 cm x 5 cm) block or a small anvil.

Nylon Mallet

Hammers and work-hardens (more on work-hardening on page 11) without changing the shape of your wire.

ROSARY PLIERS

ROUND-NOSE PLIERS

FLUSH CUTTERS

POLISHING CLOTHS

CHAIN-NOSE PLIERS

CHASING HAMMER

STEEL WOOL

COILING TOOL

BIG "DADDY" CUTTER

FILES

NYLON MALLET

TUMBLER AND
STAINLESS STEEL SHOT

Chasing Hammer

These have a ball-peen (smaller) end and a chasing (larger) end. The ball-peen end is used to flatten wire or metal and gives it a tooled appearance. The chasing hammer flattens wire without leaving hammer marks.

Polishing Cloths

I like the little white squares for an extra-shiny finish, but any polishing cloths will work.

Steel Wool

These metal scrubbing pads come in several grades. You will need a very fine grade, such as #00. This is the best tool for scouring oxidation on copper, brass, sterling, or steel.

Tumbler and Stainless Steel Shot

The best way to work-harden and clean finished jewelry. Yes, you could use your kid's rock tumbler from the craft store. You could even tumble in the washing machine. Sooner or later, you'll want to upgrade. A one-barrel tumbler should work for beginners. To tumble, place your finished jewelry and the stainless steel shot into the barrel with water and a cleaning agent (I use dish soap). As the barrel turns, the shot rubs against the metal, hardening it. At the same time, the soap polishes it clean.

Mandrels

I am all about using what you have lying around before buying special tools. If you have a selection of mandrels at your disposal, great! If not, there are other options. Steel mandrels used in beadmaking work well. Knitting needles can be mandrels for coiling and so could a small paintbrush. A large drinking glass makes for a good bracelet mandrel.

Coiling Tool

A tool for making fast, easy, and consistently sized coils.

Files

I have found my favorite file to be a simple emery board, like the ones nail artists use to file acrylic nails. (And you can get them at a dollar store!) For cleaning the edges of holes punched for wire embroidery, though, you will need a small round file. Many jewelry-supply catalogs have a simple set of starter files in a variety of shapes that will come in handy when cleaning up the edges of shapes cut out of sheet metal.

BEYOND THE BASICS

As I have said, when your skills expand, so do your tool needs. Beyond the basic tools, a few extra tools are needed for some of the projects shared in this book. I am sharing tool options for beginners as well as the possible upgrades for more experienced jewelers.

Punch Pliers

This set of pliers is essential to being able to prep metal that will be embroidered with wire. They work a lot like hole punches for paper except the holes are much smaller, and these are much stronger for piercing metal.

Replacement Punches

Sadly, the small steel screws that are used in punch pliers are only good for two or three uses (about three dozen holes) depending on how thick your metal is. Thankfully, replacements are inexpensive, and I suggest ordering extras when ordering the pliers.

TIP: Punch pliers and the replacement punches come in a few different sizes (and even shapes!). I recommend using the round 1.8 mm for the projects in this book. That goes for ordering bits for a rotary tool as well.

Rotary Tool and Bits

If you find that you fall head over heels for combining metal and wire, you may want to consider upgrading to one of these. The bits used in this type of drill are much stronger than those used in punch pliers, which means you won't need to replace the punches.

TIP: If you use a rotary tool, be sure to have a scrap piece of wood (or a bench pin) available to drill against. When the bit pushes through the metal, you will need the scrap wood to protect both yourself and your work surface.

Texture Hammers

These hammers have unique grooves and patterns on the head that leave interesting surface designs on metal. Similar in size to a chasing hammer, a texture hammer is an optional tool in the studio. You can get similar textures by finding unique metal objects around your home and using them along with a utility hammer to mar the metal's surface.

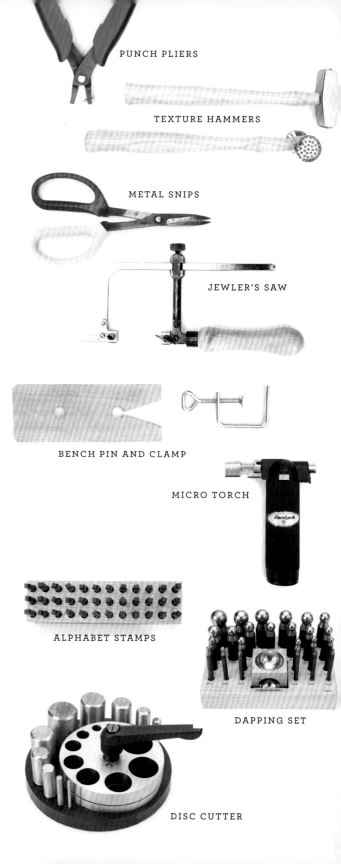

PUNCH PLIERS

TEXTURE HAMMERS

METAL SNIPS

JEWELER'S SAW

BENCH PIN AND CLAMP

MICRO TORCH

ALPHABET STAMPS

DAPPING SET

DISC CUTTER

Metal Snips

These look an awful lot like scissors, don't they? They are actually much stronger than scissors and not as sharp. These will cut sheet metal like butter but would struggle cutting a piece of yarn. They work great for cutting basic shapes out of metal.

Jeweler's Saw (and Blades)

Used to cut metal with more detail than metal snips, this tool is a standard for most metalsmiths and is becoming much more commonplace in cold-connection studios. The size of the blades varies based on the thickness of metal you need to cut.

TIP: Having good tension on your blade will lengthen the life of it. To install a blade, hold the saw between your body and a table, squeezing in just a little bit. Once the blade is in place and the screws twisted down, release the saw from your body, and you'll find the blade is nice and taut. Be sure the teeth of the blade point down toward the handle.

COLD CONNECTIONS

Wondering what a cold-connection studio is? Cold connections are metal joints made without the use of torch and solder. Something simple such as a wrapped loop or a rivet are cold connections.

Bench Pin

This simple thin piece of wood has a built-in clamp that attaches to your work surface. Bench pins give you a stable area on which to support your metal during cutting while leaving plenty of free space for your jeweler's saw to move freely. It is a must-have piece of equipment if using a jeweler's saw and should cost about $10.

Micro Torch

Fast becoming the handiest little torch in home jewelers' studios, this small handheld torch is great for drawing a bead to make your own head pins or heating copper to bring out its gorgeous red color.

good to know

Seeing this huge list of tools needed to work with metal can be a bit intimidating at first. When I was first branching out from wire-working to add more metal to my designs, I started my expanded tool collection with a jeweler's saw. Then, a few months later, I wanted to do more so I purchased my dapping set and disc cutter. More time passed before I picked up my first mirco torch and fire brick. You see, many of the tools go hand in hand, but don't need to be purchased at the same time. So don't let yourself become overwhelmed. If there is a project that really ignites your inspiration, see about getting the few extra tools for that project before getting everything listed here. Another option would be to ask if you can borrow a tool from a jewelry-making friend, to see if you like it, before buying!

Fire Brick

Slightly smaller in size than an actual building brick, but shaped the same way, these are made of an insulating fireproof material. They are very lightweight and will blacken over time with use.

Alphabet Stamps

There are dozens of different fonts available from online jewelry-supply retailers. I picked up my set at a local hardware store. This set is used to label your hardware tools.

Dapping Set

A dapping set is a collection of steel-shaping tools used with a doming block. They shape and form sheet metal.

Disc Cutter

A disc-cutting tool uses steel punches to get consistently sized metal discs from sheet metal. You can create washers by punching holes inside discs.

MANAGING *metals*

As a beginner jewelry maker, walking through the aisles of your local bead store, coming upon spools of wire and sheet metal, you can become confused and intimidated trying to discern gauges and hardness ratings and knowing which metal to use for which project. Here, we'll pull back the shroud of mystery covering both classic and alternative metals to discover their possibilities. Any of the metals I use in a given tutorial can be swapped out for another to change up the design. Once you know what metal reacts in which way, you can make the choice of what to replace that much more easily. Sterling silver will always hold a special place in my designing heart, but I must admit, I have a secret crush on sheet metal brass, and my stomach does a little flip-flop when new ideas are sparked by steel wire.

TERMINOLOGY

Before diving into all the details over what metals will do what and which sizes are best for which application, there are a few words you are going to see pop up regularly, and it is important to understand their definitions.

Wire

The stringy metal material you'll use in every project! It comes in multiple shapes, sizes, lengths, and materials. Although projects in this book use basic round wire, you should feel free to experiment with half-round, square, or other shapes of wire, if they pique your interest.

Sheet Metal

Material that has been milled into sheets (just like paper) made available in various sizes and thicknesses. When first ordering sheet metal, I recommend sticking to the basics, such as copper or brass.

Gauge

The measure of thickness for wire and sheet metal.
- 14-gauge wire makes a great core for bangles or neckwires
- 16-gauge wire is my favorite size for clasps
- 18-gauge and 20-gauge wire are excellent for making links
- 20-gauge and 21-gauge wire are standard for ear wires
- 22-gauge and 24-gauge wire are what I prefer for fine wire wrapping
- 24-gauge and 28-gauge wire work really well in wire embroidery
- 24-gauge to 30-gauge sheet metal are best for the types of projects shared in this book

Hardness

The malleability of the wire. In my experience, hardness rates are not given to sheet metal.

- Dead-soft wire is extremely malleable and can easily be bent into a myriad of shapes.
- Half-hard wire is somewhere between soft and hard; it is great for making head pins and ear wires.
- Full-hard wire is very stiff and can be difficult to work with; once formed, though, it holds its shape well under stress, making it work well for clasps.

TIP: You can always work-harden soft wire, but it takes a torch to soften (aka anneal, something beyond beginner wireworking) hard wire. I recommend buying dead-soft wire for the projects in this book.

Work-hardening

The act of making soft, malleable wire stiff through hammering or tumbling. When hammering to work-harden, you need to be careful not to hammer it to the point of becoming brittle rather than strengthened. Take a moment to pause after your first few hammer strikes; you should be able to feel the wire stiffening.

READING THE NUMBERS

The smaller the gauge number, the larger the wire or thicker the sheet metal. For example, 14-gauge wire is thicker than 24-gauge wire.

THE METALS

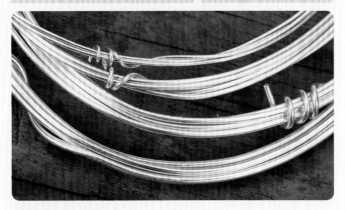

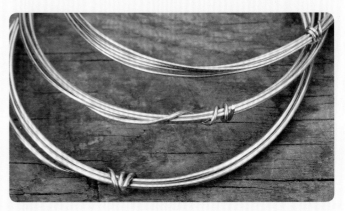

Sterling Silver

COLOR: Shiny gray/white. Will oxidize to black and can then be polished to dark gray.

MALLEABILITY: Of the metals we discuss here, sterling is the easiest to manipulate into many shapes. Easily work-hardens with hammering or tumbling.

QUALITIES: A well-respected metal for buyers. Scraps can be saved and then recycled for a monetary reimbursement (which translates to more beads in the bank, yeah!).

CONS: Costs per ounce have skyrocketed in recent years. Liver of sulfur is the only patina that will age it. Tools easily leave their mark on its surface.

Of all the metals I work with, sterling silver is really my go-to choice. Despite the cons, I love it bright, I love it oxidized, and I love how friendly it is to work with. That ever-rising cost listed under its cons has really made me have to reconsider the places I use it, though.

Copper

COLOR: Rich red/pink tones. Will oxidize to black in liver of sulfur and can then be polished to an amber brown color; also works well with heat patina (multicolored), ammonia/salt patina (blue), and vinegar/salt (green).

MALLEABILITY: This metal is noticeably stiffer than sterling but is easily manipulated into shapes. It too work-hardens easily with hammering or tumbling.

QUALITIES: Inexpensive, which makes it great for practice as well as finished pieces. Takes a variety of patinas.

CONS: People think it will turn their skin green. But with proper sealing, it won't.

Copper developed a bad reputation over the years, when wearing solid copper bangles was alleged to ease arthritis—leading to green-tinted wrists everywhere. But it was poor sealing of the metal (to protect it from the natural oils in your skin) that was to blame, not copper itself! When you work with it, remember to seal it, seal it, seal it.

good to know

When I refer to a metal as classic, it is one that average jewelry wearers have come to expect when they are purchasing a finished piece to add to their collection. Namely, these are sterling silver and gold. There are alternatives, though: copper, brass, and steel. These metals are quickly becoming just as common as the classics and rightly so. Jewelry created with these alternatives is just as beautiful and so much more affordable. For *Rustic Wrappings*, we will be focusing on the qualities of sterling, copper, brass, and steel. This quartet gracefully lends itself to the aged designs we'll be creating.

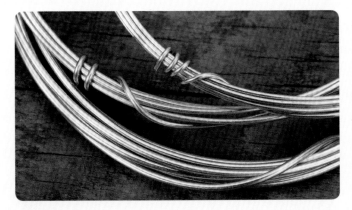

Brass

COLOR: Golden yellow. Will oxidize with ammonia fumes to a deep brown and works well with patina: ammonia/salt (blue) and vinegar/salt (green).

MALLEABILITY: Much firmer than sterling or copper. I avoid heavier gauges and stick to using 18-gauge, 20-gauge, or 22-gauge brass. Too easily work-hardens with hammering or tumbling.

QUALITIES: Beautiful golden color without the expense of real gold. Very affordable.

CONS: Doesn't easily oxidize with liver of sulfur. Most people are not as familiar with its use in jewelry.

I find myself very hard-pressed to have anything negative to say about brass, other than it is bright yellow. I am not a gold girl, and brass is so close to gold, color-wise, that I used to shy away from it. But over time, I have come to love it, especially when its deep brown and honey tones are brought out with the fumes of ammonia. Its stiffer properties are hardly noticeable once working with it for any length of time. Brass jewelry is a feast for your imagination.

Steel

COLOR: Deep gray/black.

MALLEABILITY: Very, very stiff.

QUALITIES: Least expensive of these four metals. Does not need chemicals to give a piece an oxidized appearance.

CONS: Covered in carbon that must be removed before use. Rusts easily. Must be properly sealed.

Of the four metals discussed, I deem this one the most "alternative." Steel is quickly becoming a very popular metal to work with, though, as it can be made to look very similar to oxidized sterling silver when finished. It is inexpensive—I picked up a spool of annealed (or softened) steel at my local hardware store for just $6, and there is so much wire on the spool, I am convinced it will last me my entire studio life. It comes coated in a carbon powder that needs to be removed with steel wool before using it. Exposing the steel below the carbon makes it more susceptible to rust, so like copper, sealing it is very important.

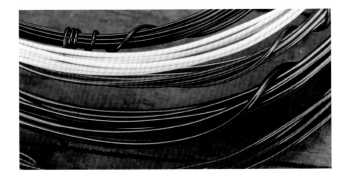

ANODIZED COLOR COPPER

This wire is a fantastic material that comes in a wide variety of colors and gauges. My personal favorites are those created by Paramount Wire. I find the finish is much more durable than others I have tried, even when hammered. Colored copper wire can be used in any tutorial shown to make a really unique finished piece of jewelry.

BASIC *techniques*

Every beautiful jewelry project begins with a solid understanding of basic techniques. I remember trying to teach myself how to make wrapped loops when I was first discovering my passion for jewelry more than nine years ago. It didn't seem so basic at the time and for the first few years, I avoided them at all cost. There is nothing like that first wrapped loop that ends up just where you want it, the size that you were hoping for. With practice, it'll become a breeze, and you will find yourself becoming more daring with your choices. How about a little bigger loop, and what about hammering the edge flat? That is when you start to have the confidence of an intermediate student, and before you know it, you will be able to see a project and know the construction without even reading the instructions, like a pro. This section is here to help you navigate the path from beginner to professional. No matter where you are on your personal jewelry journey, I think you will discover something new here.

WRAPPED LOOPS

Every tutorial I have ever seen for a wrapped loop uses multiple tools. Wrap with this, switch to that, back and forth. What a pain! My way of wrapping a loop uses just one tool. With practice, you'll get it down.

SUPPLIES: *wire, round-nose pliers, flush cutters, file*

1. Hold your wire up and down in front of you. Put your pliers in your dominant hand and hold wire about 4″ (10 cm) from the end. Your nondominant hand holds the wire in an area below the pliers. (**Figure 1**)

2. Turn your pliers away from you about 45 degrees. (**Figure 2**)

3. Use your nondominant hand to pull the bent wire around your pliers. Your pliers stay where they are while you do this. This makes a "shepherd's hook" in the wire. (**Figure 3**)

4. Take your pliers out and put them back into the shepherd's hook, but they are now up and down, not tilted back. (**Figure 4**)

5. Use your nondominant hand to pull the end of the shepherd's hook piece so that it is tight against the jaws of your pliers. It should end up behind the straight bottom piece. (**Figure 5**)

6. Wrap the straight piece two times. Look, you made a wrapped loop! (**Figure 6**)

7. Trim excess wire. File the end if sharp. (**Figure 7**)

WORKING WITH THE METALS

Each metal has its own quirks and will respond differently when used in these various techniques. Have fun experimenting and getting to know what your favorite metal is to work with!

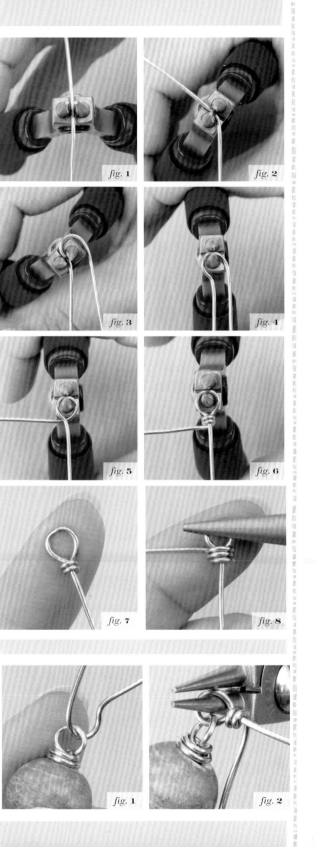

fig. 1

fig. 2

fig. 3

fig. 4

fig. 5

fig. 6

fig. 7

fig. 8

fig. 1

fig. 2

CHUNKY WRAPPED LOOPS

I love the look of these chunky wrapped loops. They look great when using a finer gauge wire with a larger bead, and they are super at hiding imperfections around a bead hole.

SUPPLIES: *wire, round-nose pliers, chain-nose pliers, flush cutters, file*

1 Follow Steps 1–6 of Wrapped Loops, but begin the first step farther down the wire leaving 6″ (15 cm) of wire for wrapping.

2 Wrap the straight piece of wire two times, closing the loop. Grip the loop with chain-nose pliers and continue wrapping the remaining wire over top of those initial wraps until you have the desired chunkiness to your wrapping. (**Figure 8**)

3 Trim excess wire. File the end if sharp.

WRAPPED-LOOP LINKS

When you are ready to move on from making a wrapped loop and want to start linking/chaining them together, it just takes one extra step. This is a technique you can use to link beads.

SUPPLIES: *wire, round-nose pliers, flush cutters, file*

1 Follow Steps 1–3 of Wrapped Loops. Before you replace your pliers so they are up and down, put a finished loop into the crook of the shepherd's hook. This locks the finished loop onto the new loop. (**Figure 1**)

2 Finish with Steps 4–7 as you would a wrapped loop. Check it out—they're linked! (**Figure 2**)

CUT YOURSELF SOME SLACK (LITERALLY)

For your first few practice loops, give yourself some extra length to do the wrapping. And if you want really consistently sized loops, mark your pliers and always wrap the marked area.

SIMPLE LOOPS

Not all loops need to be wrapped, especially when working with wire gauges as large as 16-gauge or 14-gauge. In fact, I find it almost impossible to wrap a loop with 14-gauge wire! Simple loops, sometimes called eye-pin loops, are a super alternative to wrapped loops. It can be a little tricky to get the length on these just right, but, as with everything wire-related, practice makes perfect.

SUPPLIES: *wire, flush cutters, round-nose pliers, chain-nose pliers, files*

1 Cut a piece of wire about 2" (5 cm) and file one end.

2 Using round-nose pliers, bend the filed end of wire so that it forms a letter P. (**Figure 1**)

3 Use your chain-nose pliers to grasp the P just inside the loop where the end meets the straight length of wire. Bend the loop, making it sit up and look like a lollipop. (**Figure 2**)

4 Slide on your bead and repeat on the other end. This time, cut the wire to about ¾" (2 cm), file, and use chain-nose pliers to make a 45-degree bend. (**Figure 3**)

5 Use round-nose pliers to roll the filed end in toward the bead. (**Figure 4**)

SPIRALS

Spirals are a great, versatile item that should be in every wireworker's repertoire. Make them with a simple loop for cute dangles or make them on the end of head pins. The possibilities are endless.

SUPPLIES: *wire, flush cutter, file, round-nose pliers, chain-nose pliers*

1 Flush cut and file one end of a length of wire.

2 For an open spiral or closed spiral: using the tip of your round-nose pliers, start to bend the end of wire. *Make sure the end of your wire is flush to your round-nose pliers' shaft. If it extends out, you'll get a bump in your spiral. (**Figure 1**)

3 Before this first wrap of spiral reaches the straight portion of your wire, stop. If you go too far, you'll be making an egg-shaped spiral instead of a pretty round one.

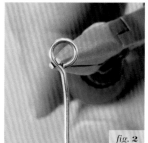

fig. 1   *fig. 2*

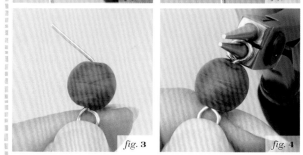

fig. 3   *fig. 4*

CUT YOURSELF SOME SLACK (FIGURATIVELY)

Remember, if you are a beginner, don't get frustrated if your wrapped loop didn't turn out perfect. These take practice. Your 10th will be better than your first and your 100th will be better then your 10th. You have to keep at it!

fig. 1

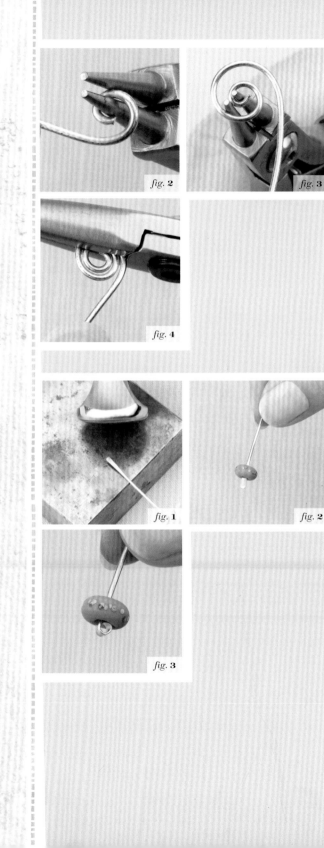

fig. 2

fig. 3

fig. 4

fig. 1

fig. 2

fig. 3

You need to think of this as a spiral, not a circle. Guide the straight length of wire around the outside of the starter loop. (**Figure 2**)

Open Spiral

4 Use the natural resistance of the wire to form the open spiral shape. Wire likes to be round, and it'll spiral nicely if you don't try to force it. Twist your pliers as needed to keep the jaw tips out of the way of your spiral. (**Figure 3**)

Closed Spiral

4 To have a tighter closed spiral, you'll need to switch to chain-nose pliers after the initial wrap. Use the base of the pliers and grasp the spiral area. Use your other hand to guide the straight end into the spiral until you reach the size you need. (**Figure 4**)

TIP: It never hurts to set the pliers down and do some spiraling with your hands.

HEAD PINS

Head pins are a jewelry-making staple, and making your own is a breeze. You can make them simple or doll them up with spirals or try your hand at balling the metal on the end of the wire with a micro torch (see page 19). The possibilities are endless, and you really can't go wrong.

Easy Head Pin

SUPPLIES: *wire, flush cutters, file, bench block, chasing hammer, round-nose pliers*

1 Cut wire to 2–3" (5–7.5 cm) lengths. (Length will vary depending on your project.) File ends.

2 With the chasing end of your hammer, flatten about ¼" (6 mm) of one end of your wire piece against your bench block. (**Figure 1**)

3 If your bead hole is small, you can leave the head pin like this (**Figure 2**); or, using the tip of your round-nose pliers, roll back the flattened end (**Figure 3**). You're done!

Shaped Head Pin

SUPPLIES: *wire, flush cutters, file, bench block, chasing hammer, round-nose pliers, chain-nose pliers*

1   Using a piece of wire 2½–3½" (6.5–9 cm), begin by flush cutting and filing smooth one end of the wire.

2   With the tip of your round-nose pliers, grasp the filed end of wire and start to twist it into a spiral. (See instructions for Spirals on page 16.) Stop when the jaws of your pliers get in the way of forming the spiral and switch to chain-nose pliers.

3   When your spiral is the size you want it, use your chain-nose pliers to form a 90-degree bend in the straight area of wire at the area nearest your spiral. (**Figure 1**)

4   (Optional) To add a little interest to your head pin, you can use a chasing hammer and bench block to flatten the spiral just made. (**Figure 2**)

Flat Spiral Head Pin

This style head pin is great for those times when you want to hide the head of the head pin. These hug tight to the underside of your heads and nearly disappear when used in dangles.

SUPPLIES: *18-gauge wire, chain-nose pliers*

1   About 2" (5 cm) from one end of a 5" (12.7 cm) piece of 18-gauge wire, use the chain-nose pliers to form a 90-degree angle in the wire. (**Figure 1**)

2   Grasp the longer end of wire close to the angle and working from the center out, start to form a tight spiral (**Figure 2**). After starting, you may need to switch the position of your pliers so that they grab the outer edge of the spiral (**Figure 3**).

3   Continue building the spiral until it is your desired size (usually two full loops is enough). Trim excess wire and file smooth. (**Figure 4**)

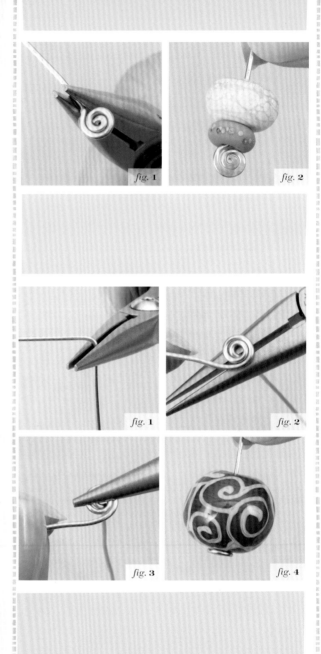

fig. 1

fig. 2

fig. 1

fig. 2

fig. 3

fig. 4

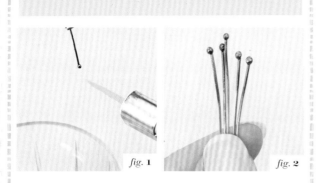

fig. 1   fig. 2

BEAD PLUS FLAME EQUALS BAD

Glass beads should never be near an open flame. Rapidly changing temperature causes thermal shock in glass and will lead to the bead breaking or even shattering. So, don't be tempted to create a link, slip on a glass bead, and draw a bead on the end of the wire. The glass bead won't survive.

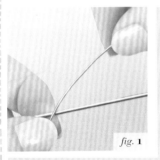

fig. 1

DON'T SCRAP YOUR SCRAPS

Save your coil scraps. They make great fillers in other projects!

Drawing a Bead

I was a little nervous the first time I drew a bead—heating the metal so hot it balls up on the end of the wire. But as soon as I made that first one, it was love at first bead. These are so easy, and making your own can really save money. It is important to work on a clean, stable, heat-proof work surface (a baking sheet on the kitchen counter is a great place). To be extra safe, have a fire extinguisher nearby.

SUPPLIES: *20-gauge wire, chain-nose pliers, micro torch, bowl with water*

1   Have several pieces of wire cut to 3" (7.5 cm) lengths ready to go on your work surface. Light your torch.

2   Hold your wire vertically in the flame with your pliers. The wire will begin to glow red and ball up on itself. (**Figure 1**)

3   Once the bead is formed, remove the wire from the flame and plunge it into the bowl of water.

4   Repeat for as many head pins as you'd like! (**Figure 2**)

COILING

One of these days I am going to have a bumper sticker printed that says "Coiling ROCKS!" Coiling wire is my go-to technique for almost every project I create. It can add substance, interest, depth, texture, and even color to a design nearly effortlessly.

SUPPLIES: *20-gauge wire, steel mandrel, flush cutters*

1   The length and gauge of wire used to make a coil will greatly change the finished length of coil. To practice the technique, start with a 2' (61 cm) length of 20-gauge wire around a ³⁄₃₂" (2.5 mm) mandrel. Your finished coil should be about 2" (5 cm) long.

2   Hold the mandrel in your nondominant hand. Pinch your wire piece against the mandrel between your thumb and forefinger about 1" (2.5 cm) from the end. Grasp the long side of wire with your dominant hand about 8" (20.5 cm) from the mandrel. (**Figure 1**)

3   Start wrapping the wire around the mandrel. Work slowly at first to keep the wraps tight. As you get into the rhythm of wrapping, you'll start to move faster.

As you go, loosen your grip on the wire in your dominant hand to keep your hand about 6″ (15 cm) from the mandrel. (**Figure 2**)

TIP: If you get gaps in the coil, use chain-nose pliers to squeeze the gaps together as you go.

4   Once you get about 1″ (2.5 cm) from the end, flush cut the end of coiled wire. Go back and flush cut any excess at the start of your coil, too. Slide it off the mandrel and you are ready to use it. (**Figure 3**)

FABRICATING FINDINGS

Components used to create jewelry are called findings. Jump rings, clasps, and earring wires are just a few jewelry findings that you can create yourself. Granted, they can be purchased in mass quantities at minimal expense, but finishing off a wonderful handmade piece of jewelry with a premade lobster clasp really seems a shame to me. The following are a few easy finding techniques to add to your skill set.

Jump Rings

Coils can easily become jump rings!

SUPPLIES: *16-gauge wire, steel mandrel, flush cutters, chain-nose pliers*

1   Use the same technique explained in the coiling section (see page 19) with 16-gauge wire around a ¼″ (6 mm) mandrel.

2   After slipping the finished coil off the mandrel, stretch it slightly (**Figure 1**) and use the flush cutters or big daddy cutter to cut rings from the coil (**Figure 2**).

3   Use two sets of chain-nose pliers to open and close the rings. Slightly twist them open and shut (**Figures 3 and 4**)—don't open them wide and pinch them shut.

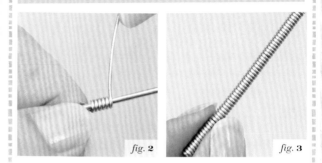

fig. 2   fig. 3

USING THE GIZMO

I think the Coiling Gizmo is great! I love using mine for long coils more then 3″ (7.5 cm). Anything else I do by hand. Directions for creating coils should be included with your gizmo.

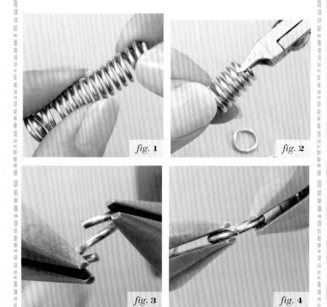

fig. 1   fig. 2

fig. 3   fig. 4

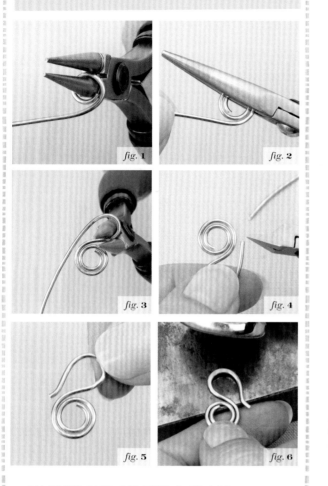

fig. 1   fig. 2

fig. 3   fig. 4

fig. 5   fig. 6

VARIATIONS ON THE S-CLASP

There are countless variations that can be made of the simple S-clasp. Try making the starting loop small and the hook larger, or vice versa. You can even leave a little length between the starting loop and the hook to wrap a bit of extra wire.

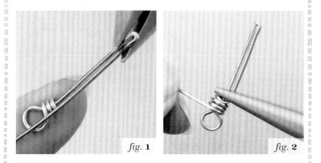

fig. 1   fig. 2

Clasps

Most projects will need a clasp of some sort to close them. You can make a bunch ahead of time and have them waiting for projects or make them as needed. These are three very basic clasps to get you started.

SIMPLE S-CLASP

SUPPLIES: *16-gauge wire, flush cutters, file, round-nose pliers, chain-nose pliers, nylon mallet/chasing hammer, bench block*

1 Begin this clasp by cutting a 5" (12.5 cm) length of 16-gauge wire. Flush cut and file one end.

2 Using the very base of your round-nose pliers, start a closed spiral that has a large hole in the center (**Figure 1**). Switch to your chain-nose pliers, if needed, to complete the second wrap of the coil (**Figure 2**).

3 Reposition your pliers to form an arch/hook into the other end of the coiled piece of wire. (**Figure 3**)

4 Use the center of your coil hole to judge where to trim the excess of your hook end. Line up with the center of that hole, flush cut, and file the end. (**Figure 4**)

5 Use chain-nose pliers to bend the flush cut end back on itself. (**Figure 5**)

6 Work-harden the arch of the hook and the coiled area. Use the chasing hammer if you want a flattened arch or use your nylon mallet to leave it as is. (**Figure 6**)

BASIC HOOK CLASP

SUPPLIES: *wire, flush cutters, round-nose pliers, chain-nose pliers, files*

1 Cut an 8" (20.5 cm) piece of 18-gauge wire. Make a wrapped loop (see page 15).

2 About 1" (2.5 cm) from the wrapped loop, fold the wire over on itself. Use your chain-nose pliers to get a tight bend. The pieces should be running side by side. (**Figure 1**)

3 Use your chain-nose pliers to grasp the parallel pieces of wire close to the wrapped loop from Step 2. Using your free hand, wrap the longer wire with the shorter wire as shown. Trim excess wire. (**Figure 2**)

4 Using round-nose pliers, form a bend in the parallel wires to make a hook. (**Figure 3**)

5 Tumble finished clasps to work-harden.

TOGGLE CLASP

This is a two-part clasp. One side is a large loop that the other side slides into. Toggles are fabulously trendy, and this is an easy one to make. I have heard complaints that toggles easily come loose when being worn, leading to lost bracelets around the world. If you make sure the toggle bar is long enough, it won't slip out!

SUPPLIES: *16-gauge wire, file, flush cutters, mandrel, round-nose pliers, chain-nose pliers, chasing hammer/nylon mallet, bench block, tumbler*

1 Cut two pieces of 16-gauge wire to 3" (7.5 cm). Flush cut and file both ends.

2 Start with the loop end of the toggle. Use a child's marker or other mandrel about ½" (1.3 cm) in diameter to wrap the filed end of wire around. This forms a large loop on one end. (**Figure 1**)

3 With round-nose pliers, bend the opposite end of wire, forming a figure eight. One end can be larger than the other. Work-harden with a bench block and mallet if desired. Set aside. (**Figure 2**)

4 Pick up the second piece of wire. This will make the "through" end of the toggle. Using your round-nose pliers, hold the wire at the center and pull the wire ends in opposite directions, creating a loop in the center of the wire. (**Figure 3**)

5 Using the flush cutters, trim the straight lengths of wire to equal lengths and file if needed. Then, use the chasing hammer and bench block to flatten the cut ends. (**Figure 4**)

6 Work-harden the clasp by tumbling in a tumbler or by using a bench block and mallet.

fig. 3

ROCK THE CLASP

I like to think of clasps as a signature for your jewelry. Find a style of clasp you love and use it all the time.

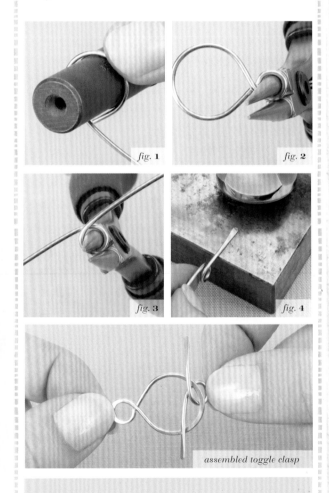

fig. 1

fig. 2

fig. 3

fig. 4

assembled toggle clasp

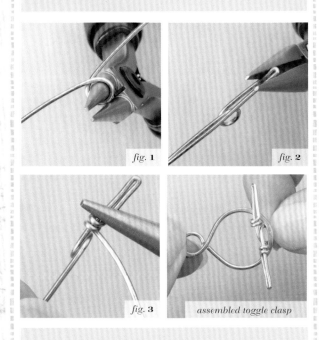

fig. 1

fig. 2

fig. 3

assembled toggle clasp

GENTLE ON YOUR EARS

Earlobes can be sensitive, but most people won't have a reaction to the metal. If you know your wearer can handle different metal alloys, then feel free to make earring wires from copper or brass, too!

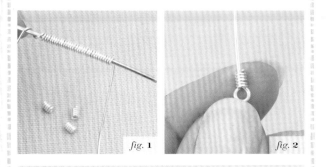

fig. 1

fig. 2

ANOTHER TOGGLE

SUPPLIES: *18-gauge wire, flush cutters, round-nose pliers, chain-nose pliers, tumbler*

1 From a 6″ (15 cm) piece of 18-gauge wire, use round-nose pliers to make a loop in the center of the wire. This will be the loop that lets you attach your toggle bar to your jewelry. (**Figure 1**)

2 Mark each straight piece of the wire about ½″ (1.3 cm) from the center where the loop is. Use chain-nose pliers to fold the wire back on itself. It should look like two pieces of wire are running parallel to each other. Pinch the fold in the wire with your chain-nose pliers to make a tight hairpin-style bend. (**Figure 2**)

3 Grasp the parallel wire and wrap the free end of wire over the other as if closing a wrapped loop. (**Figure 3**)

4 Repeat these steps for the opposite side of the toggle.

5 Work-harden in a rotary tumbler for 30 minutes.

Earring Wires

I consider clasps to be the finishing touch to necklaces, and ear wires are most certainly the finishing touch for earrings. A great ear wire can really set an earring design apart from the crowd. Learn these few basic designs and down the road you'll be free to let your imagination run wild with funkier shapes.

FISHHOOK-STYLE EAR WIRES

This is a classic style of ear hooks. They are effortless to make, and I suggest making several dozen at once so they are ready to use when you need them.

SUPPLIES: *24-gauge wire, thin mandrel, 20-gauge wire, flush cutters, file, round-nose pliers, chain-nose pliers, a round pencil, tumbler, chasing hammer, bench block*

1 Start by coiling 24-gauge wire around a thin (¹⁄₁₆″ [1.5 mm] or scrap of 18-gauge wire) mandrel. Remove the coiled piece from the mandrel and trim into small equally sized pieces. They should be about five wraps each. (**Figure 1**)

2 Cut several pieces of 20-gauge wire to 3″ (7.5 cm) lengths. Flush cut and file one end of each piece.

3 Starting at the filed end, create a small simple loop (see page 16) with the tip of your round-nose pliers. Slide on one of the small coil tube beads you made in Step 1. (**Figure 2**)

4 With chain-nose pliers, grasp the ear wire tight, with your pliers firmly against the coil bead. Bend a 45-degree angle in the wire. (**Figure 3**)

5 Wrap the straight end around a round pencil or ¼" (6 mm) mandrel. This gives you a nice consistent arch so all your hooks match. (**Figure 4**)

TIP: If you always use the same tool to form your ear wires, the hooks will always be the same size!

6 Measure about 1" (2.5 cm) from the top of the arch and trim excess wire. Flush cut, and file the end. Use the tip of your chain-nose pliers to put a little bend in the end of your wire about ⅛" (3 mm) from the end. (**Figure 5**)

7 Using the chasing end of your hammer and bench block, flatten the arch of your hook slightly. (**Figure 6**)

8 Tumble hooks in a rotary tumbler for about 30 minutes to work-harden and polish. When you are ready to use your hook, open the loop and add your dangle.

FRENCH EAR WIRES

Want to add a little drama to your hooks? Go for the large loopiness of French-style ear hooks.

SUPPLIES: *20-gauge wire, flush cutter, file, chasing hammer, bench block, round-nose pliers, large round mandrel (about 1" [2.5 cm] diameter), chain-nose pliers, rotary tumbler*

1 Get these ear wires started by flush cutting and filing the ends on 2" (5 cm) pieces of 20-gauge wire. Use your chasing hammer to flatten the first ¼" (6 mm) on one end of each piece. (See head pins on page 17.)

2 Using your round-nose pliers, create a loop with the flattened area of wire. Treat this how you would the start of an open or closed coil. You want to tuck the end of the loop in and bring the straight piece out and around the loop. (**Figure 1**)

3 Wrap the straight piece of wire around a large mandrel. Use your imagination and look for something around the house that will work (e.g., one of those extra-large permanent markers or a bottle of nail polish). You want to wrap all the way around so that it creates a loop that is about three-quarters of the way around your mandrel. (**Figure 2**)

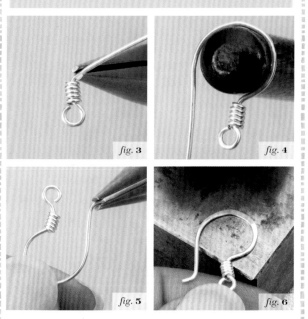

fig. 3 *fig. 4* *fig. 5* *fig. 6*

VARIATIONS ON FISHHOOK EAR WIRES

Exaggerating or minimizing the size of the hook that rests in your ear can really change the look. All use the same technique as shared above; just change the placement of the arch!

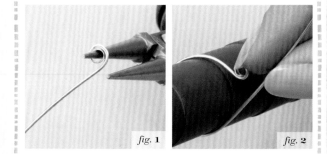

fig. 1 *fig. 2*

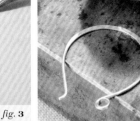

fig. 3

fig. 4

assembled French ear wire

IT'S HOOP TO BE SQUARE

Hoops don't have to be round! You can make them oval or triangular or any other shape.

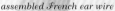

fig. 1

fig. 2

assembled hoop ear wire

4 With your chain-nose pliers, put a little bend in the end of the wire and trim it. Be sure to flush cut and file your end, too. (**Figure 3**)

5 These ear wires need work-hardening, just like everything else. You can tumble them in a rotary tumbler or hammer them with a chasing hammer/nylon mallet, depending on the look you are going for. (**Figure 4**)

HOOP EAR WIRES

Hoops seem to be a fickle style of ear wire: one year they are hot, the next year not so much. One thing is for sure, though—they always come back into fashion. Make a pair and wear them today; perhaps you'll be the next trendsetter.

SUPPLIES: *wire, flush cutters, round-nose pliers, mandrel, chain-nose pliers, chasing hammer, bench block, tumbler*

1 You will need two pieces of wire 3" (7.5 cm) long. Flush cut and file one end. Then, using round-nose pliers, form a simple loop at that end. (See page 16, simple loops.)

2 Wrap the wire around a mandrel a little smaller than the size you want your finished loop to be. (The wire will tend to spring back a bit when off the mandrel, making it just a bit larger.)

3 With your chasing hammer and bench block, flatten the hoop of wire. (**Figure 1**)

4 Trim the longer end of wire so that it is about ⅛" (2 mm) longer than needed. File this end and use chain-nose pliers to form a slight bend where the end meets the simple loop. This end should easily slip into the simple loop. Repeat for the second ear wire. (**Figure 2**)

5 Tumble hooks in a rotary tumbler for about 30 minutes to work-harden and polish.

patina recipes

and

SEALING SOLUTIONS

Each time I enter my studio and begin to pull together the ingredients needed for one of these patina recipes, I feel a bit like a baker in the kitchen. So many of the elements used are common household items, found in your pantry or right under the sink. As with all recipes, add a pinch of this or a dash of that and you get a new look each time.

PREPARING THE METAL

For all the following patina recipes, the metal is prepped in the same way. It is important to do any forming and shaping of the metal before prepping it for the finished patina. Patinas can chip or be rubbed away if you attempt to further hammer, or bend, or manipulate the metal once the patina is applied. Once the metal is formed, it should be thoroughly cleaned to remove any residual oils from your skin or any coating that may have been applied by the supplier. A light sanding with steel wool followed by a washing with salt water is the best way to do this. Dry the metal after cleaning and your components are ready to accept the patina.

LIVER OF SULFUR (LOS): *the traditional oxidized patina*

SUPPLIES: *water, liver of sulfur, glass dish or other container, baking soda, polishing cloth*

USED ON: *sterling silver, copper*

Most wireworkers and jewelry makers quickly learn that the best way to darken the metal they use in their designs is with liver of sulfur (LOS). It is by far the most tried-and-true method of oxidizing metal. It doesn't work on every metal, though—and this probably isn't already under your kitchen sink. LOS can be purchased online or in the stained-glass department of craft stores, as it is traditionally used to darken the metal that runs between the panes of glass in stained-glass creations.

Liver of sulfur comes in three forms: liquid, gel, or solid chunks. I prefer the liquid form, but it can dry out over time if you don't use it very often. Consider yourself warned that no matter what form you use it in, it stinks! Before disposing of it, you should neutralize it with baking soda. Just stir in 1 tablespoon of baking soda and then pour it down the sink. You can also flush it down the toilet if you'd rather not have the odor linger in your kitchen.

1 Dissolve 1 teaspoon of liquid LOS and 2 cups warm water in a glass bowl.

2 Submerge your wire in the LOS solution until blackened.

3 Remove from the liquid and dry. Then use a polishing cloth to remove the tarnish on the surface. The deeper areas will remain blackened, giving the metal depth.

4 It isn't necessary to seal this patina if using sterling silver, but you should seal copper that will come in contact with skin. Seal your patina on copper using wax.

TIP: Brass does not oxidize in LOS.

OXIDIZED PATINA FOR BRASS

SUPPLIES: *ammonia, resealable bag, cotton balls, polishing cloth*

USED ON: *brass*

Attempting to oxidize brass with LOS as you do sterling silver or copper can be a tedious task. The process varies from very, very slow to nonexistent. It is much easier to oxidize brass with ammonia fumes. It is fast, it is easy, and the results are fantastic every time.

1 Moisten two or three cotton balls with ammonia and place in a resealable plastic bag.

2 Place your brass jewelry inside the bag with the cotton balls and seal the bag closed.

3 Allow to oxidize for 30 minutes to 1 hour until the brass appears to be a dark brown or black color. Remove brass from the bag and polish back the tarnish.

4 Brass oxidized in this way does not need to be sealed.

TIP: Keep the bag with your ammonia-soaked cotton balls tightly sealed when not in use, and you can reuse it several times before needing to replace the cotton balls.

HEAT PATINA

SUPPLIES: *micro torch, fire brick*

USED ON: *copper, brass*

High temperatures can bring out a really beautiful random variety of color on the surface of copper and brass. The look takes seconds to achieve and brings a one-of-a-kind quality to each piece you create with heat. Be sure to keep studio safety in mind; you should have a fire extinguisher nearby any time you are working with an open flame. Also, keep a bowl of water on your workbench to quench metal that has become overheated. You'll know you have gone too far with the heat if the metal turns a dark brown, or black, burnt color.

1. Place your metal components on a fire brick on a heat-proof work surface.

2. Light your micro torch and quickly pass the flame back and forth over the metal (also known as flashing). You should see color start to bloom on the surface of the metal. It is very important to keep your flame moving. Never focus in one place for too long—doing so will create fire scale, a yucky black look that takes effort to remove.

3. Remove the heat and allow the metal to cool.

4. Seal this patina with wax or Permalac.

TIP: Quenching the metal in water after bringing the color to the surface tends to dull the colors. I get the best results by letting the metal naturally cool down.

AMMONIA AND SALT WATER PATINA

SAVING FACE (AND BRAIN)

WARNING! Ammonia is a harsh chemical with extremely pungent fumes. Work in a well-ventilated area while using ammonia and wear protective gloves.

SUPPLIES: *ammonia, salt water, resealable container, smaller bowl that fits inside of container, plastic mesh, spritzer*

USED ON: *copper, brass*

I was first introduced to this form of patina in Linda and Opie O'Brien's book, *Metal Craft Discovery Workshop* (North Light Books, 2005). Using their technique as a platform, I jumped into my own experiments with ammonia and salt water. I discovered that my favorite patina is created when adding spritzes of salt water directly to the surface of the metal after washing it. The results are a richer blue color and a dappled effect. The sealer you choose for this patina is important as some can dilute the color, change it, or make it disappear completely.

1. Pour about ½" (1.3 cm) of ammonia into a small open container and place it inside a larger resealable container. Lay a piece of plastic mesh on top of the inner container.

2. Lay your metal components on the mesh and then spritz with salt water.

3 Close the lid tightly and allow patina to develop. The amount of time the patina is allowed to develop will greatly change the finished level of color. The longer you leave it, the bluer it will become.

4 After an extended period of time, remove the metal component from the sealed container. It will have a dark brown hue with subtle hints of blue. Allow to air-dry and bold blue color will appear.

5 Seal this patina with Permalac; water-based sealers will turn this finish a cloudy white.

RECYCLE IT

This setup is reusable! Keep the lid tightly sealed and you can reuse this method time and time again.

VINEGAR PATINA

SUPPLIES: *white vinegar, sawdust, resealable container, paintbrush*

USED ON: *copper, brass*

Where ammonia turns most metals blue, vinegar takes them to a lovely place where green grows. Unlike ammonia, however, the fumes don't cause the effect; you can't simply soak a piece in vinegar to get the look, either. Instead, you need something to hold the moisture of the vinegar and let it wick down onto the metal. I have exper-imented with several mediums to see which works best for this. By far, I have had the most success with sawdust. The fine shavings of wood leave behind an almost crystalline sheen to the surface of the metal that reminds me of The Emerald City in *The Wizard of Oz*.

1 Fill a small resealable container with sawdust.

2 Pour a liberal amount of white vinegar on the sawdust and mix with your fingers. Not all the dust needs to be soaked, but it should start to come together almost like a paste.

3 Bury your metal in the saturated sawdust and seal the container. Allow to set overnight.

TIP: If you can create a greenhouse environment by putting the sealed container in direct sunlight, you can greatly speed up the process. The intense heat helps hasten the patina development.

4 Remove the metal components from the sawdust and let air-dry. Once dry, use a soft bristle brush to gently remove any sawdust stuck to the surface of the metal. Don't concern yourself with removing every single piece of sawdust. When the patina is sealed, the remnants add to the texture of the surface and aged feel of the piece.

5 Seal this patina with Permalac.

POTATO CHIP PATINA

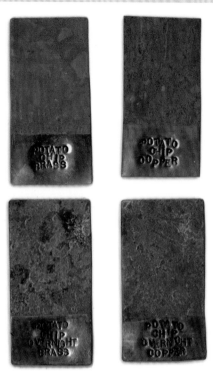

SUPPLIES: *salt-and-vinegar potato chips, white vinegar, resealable container, paintbrush*

USED ON: *copper, brass*

Yep, the rumors are true! You can patina metal with salt-and-vinegar potato chips. The resulting effect is unique, and the conversations you'll have when explaining it to admirers of your jewelry will be, too. The longer you can leave your metal buried in this snack, the more pronounced the patina will be. The only downsides to this method are that you can't eat the chips after creating the patina, and you can't save them to reuse—they will mold.

1   Crush several handfuls of salt-and-vinegar potato chips into a resealable container.

2   Pour white vinegar over the chips and mash and mix them until moistened and mushy.

3   Bury your metal components into the mushy chips and make sure the metal is completely covered. Seal the container.

4   Allow the patina to develop. The longer you leave the metal under the surface of the chips, the more green will grow. Samples show metal left for 1 hour versus leaving it overnight.

5   Remove metal from the chip mixture and allow it to air-dry. When dry, you can use a soft bristled brush to remove any chips still stuck to the surface. Discard the chip mixture after the first use.

6   Seal this patina with Permalac.

good to know

Commercial patinas are becoming more and more readily available in the metal market-place. These are premixed liquid solutions to apply to metal and can be left to react either naturally or with heat, giving your metal even more aged color options, such as a rusted look that is a rich red color. For *Rustic Wrappings*, I have chosen to focus on patina that you can make yourself with household items. As always, though, once you are comfortable with these processes, I encourage you expand your patina knowledge and experiment with commercial applied patina. Be sure to carefully read any instructions provided by the manufacturer and follow all safety guidelines.

ALCOHOL INK PATINA

SUPPLIES: *alcohol inks, gesso, polishing cloth, paintbrush*

USED ON: *any metal*

I often debate with myself as to the merits of this technique being called a patina or simply a really cool trick. Unlike the other patina recipes, this no-bake recipe gives instant results. And there are so many possibilities to the colors that can be bestowed onto the surfaces of both metal and wire. This works best with textured or patterned metal, as the color needs some place to set and have some contrast with the highlighted areas, which is one of the reasons it looks especially beautiful on wire coils.

1 Working on a craft mat, use a paintbrush to apply a thin coat of a gesso or other white paint to the surface of your metal and allow to dry.

TIP: For a darker color effect, skip Step 1 and go directly to Step 2.

2 Drip droplets of different color inks onto the painted metal and allow to dry.

3 You can leave the effect as is, or use very fine sandpaper to polish back the raised surfaces of the metal for contrast before sealing.

4 Seal this patina with Permalac or Mod Podge.

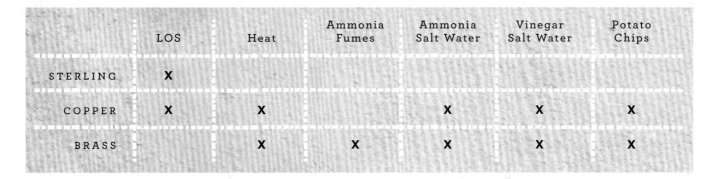

	LOS	Heat	Ammonia Fumes	Ammonia Salt Water	Vinegar Salt Water	Potato Chips
STERLING	X					
COPPER	X	X		X	X	X
BRASS		X	X	X	X	X

RUSTING

SUPPLIES: *hydrogen peroxide, white vinegar, salt, small dish or container*

USED ON: *steel*

In most cases, you aren't going to want to have rusted steel in your projects, but it can actually be a really cool look for earrings. However, you don't need to leave your earrings out in the rain for weeks waiting for the rust to form! It is easy to accelerate the rusting process with just a few simple steps.

1 Mix equal parts hydrogen peroxide (the kind you can get at your local pharmacy) and white vinegar. Stir in ½ teaspoon of salt.

2 Dip steel into the solution and allow rust to form. Remember, your metal should already be shaped before applying the patina.

3 Remove from the patina and allow to dry.

4 Seal this patina with Permalac or Mod Podge.

TIP: This patina can easily chip or flake off, which is why I recommend it for earrings as they are a piece of jewelry that isn't overly played with while worn.

SEALANTS: *protecting the patina*

I can't tell you enough how essential it is to seal your patina. Let me say it again: you must seal your patina! Not only will it protect the patina on your jewelry and give the piece a longer life, but it also will protect the skin of the person wearing the piece from any residual chemical that may still be on the surface of the metal.

Sealing your metal jewelry is simple and you have dozens of products to choose from when it comes to picking sealants. Everyone has a favorite. So, if you find you don't like what I like, try some others and find what works best for you. Whatever you choose, remember, always seal your patina!

Wax

USED ON: *LOS, heat*

Renaissance is the most commonly used wax sealer and is used primarily to keep rust from forming on steel. It can also be rubbed onto the surface of oxidized copper and brass to slow the natural aging process. If a particular piece of jewelry is worn frequently, you may need to reapply a layer of wax from time to time.

Craft Sealers

USED ON: *alcohol ink, rust*

Mod Podge is the most popular craft water-based sealer/glue/finish on the market. It is available is matte and gloss luster, which are nice options to have depending on the finished look you are going for. It can be used to seal alcohol ink patina and vinegar-based patinas, but I do not recommend it for ammonia-based ones.

Aerosol Spray Sealers

USED ON: *any patina*

Many jewelry makers prefer Permalac, a sealant designed specifically to protect metal. Spray sealant is a must for sealing patina that has been applied to a chain or for those projects where a brushstroke could damage the patina. Several thin coats will yield a much better result than one thick coat. Have patience and allow each layer to dry thoroughly and you will have a beautiful finished piece of jewelry.

wire EMBROIDERY

The art of wire embroidery is one I stumbled upon while out book browsing with a friend. We were in the craft section, and as I flipped through the pages of several embroidery books, a light went on in my head. What if I embroidered with wire instead of floss? I began experimenting in my studio and kept the techniques a secret close to my heart, waiting to share it with everyone in this book.

In this chapter, I have really only scratched the surface of possibilities that wire embroidery offers. Keep the stitching simple to make projects that are very quick and gratifying without a lot of frustration. For those with the patience to carry out complex designs, the sky is the limit.

THE PROCESS

SUPPLIES: *24-gauge wire, punch pliers, chain-nose pliers, round-nose pliers, flush cutters, precut metal blanks or sheet metal, pencil, files*

Step 1: The Design

Unlike other forms of jewelry making that are best left to a more random, organic design process, wire embroidery is one that needs a bit of planning. Take the time to sketch your ideas for a finished piece.

Once you know just what you want to embroider onto your metal component, it needs to be transferred from the planning page to your actual metal piece. This can be as simple as redrawing it with a pencil, or you can make a laser photocopy of your sketch and use heat and burnishing tools to transfer the image to the metal. Personally, I go for the pencil option every time.

Step 2: Piercing the Metal

With the sketch in place, use punch pliers to pierce the metal in the places where your wire will travel from the front of your work to the back. If the punch pliers leave a rough edge to the back side of the hole, use a file to clean up the metal. This is important, since any rough edge will run the risk of scarring the surface of your wire as it passes through the hole.

Step 3: Embroider

Now for the fun part. Your design is set, your holes are punched, and all that is left to do is to work your wire in and out through the holes to create the finished design. You need to anchor a small tail of the wire to the back side before passing it through the first hole. Unlike traditional embroidery, no knot is needed in the wire to anchor it—a simple bend, or a small spiral in the wire, against the back of the metal will hold it in place.

Work with lengths of wire that are comfortable for you. Since you can anchor your wire on the back side of your work at any time, you don't need to try to work with a wire that is extremely long.

I find the best gauges of wire for embroidering are 24 and 26. Thicker wire would need larger holes to work with, distracting from the design, and finer wire tends to break when tugged on too hard.

TRADITIONAL STITCHES

Similar to how all wireworking pieces use a few simple techniques, most embroidered designs are the result of a few basic stitches. You can get in some great practice and familiarize yourself with these basic stitches by creating a sampler of sorts in the form of stitched metal strips. Needlework samplers were quite popular years ago and were a way for a woman to show off her stitching skills. I love having these sampler strips in my studio as not only a reference but as conversation pieces, too.

SUPPLIES: *24-gauge or 26-gauge wire, punch pliers, chain-nose pliers, round-nose pliers, flush cutters, precut metal blanks or sheet metal, pencil, files*

Running Stitch

1 Using punch pliers, create a series of holes ¼" (6 mm) apart along the length of a piece of sheet metal.

2 Anchor the end of a 12" (30.5 cm) piece of wire to the back side of your work.

3 Thread the wire in and out of the holes, creating an over-and-under-looking pattern to the wire. This stitch should look the same on the front and the back of the work. Finish by anchoring the wire.

TIP: Look for ways to be creative when anchoring your wire tail. In this sample, I anchored the wire on the front of the work with a simple spiral of wire.

TRUST THE TEMPLATE

In Rustic Wrappings, *all embroidered designs have detailed drawings that you can copy and transfer to your metal.*

MIXING PATINA AND WIRE EMBROIDERY

When wanting to create a finished piece with lots of visual interest, you'll want to mix both the look of a patina and wire embroidery. But which should you do first? Begin by laying out the design, then piercing the holes. Follow that with applying the patina and sealing it and finish with the wire embroidery.

Backstitch

1 This stitch begins the same as the others with a series of holes created with punch pliers about ¼" (6 mm) apart on a length of sheet metal.

2 Anchor the end of a 24" (61 cm) piece of wire to the back side of your work. Pass the wire from the front of your work to the back through the second hole.

3 Come back up through the third hole and then pass your wire back into the second hole.

4 From the back of your work, bring the wire up through the fourth hole and then back through the third. You should start to be able to see the continuous line that this stitch creates.

5 Continue repeating Steps 3 and 4, progressing through the rest of the holes until you reach the end of your work. Anchor the tail wire to the back of your piece.

Chain Stitch

1 Using punch pliers, create a series of holes about ¼" (6 mm) apart along a length of a piece of sheet metal. Changing the distance between holes will change the look of your finished design.

2 Using a 24" (61 cm) piece of 24-gauge wire, pass both ends of wire through the front of your work to the back of your work. Leave about ¼" (6 mm) of the loop on the front side and anchor the wire to the back of the work with a shorter end of wire. The long length of wire will be used to embroider the stitches. Press the wire loop flat against the sheet metal.

3 Pass the longer end of wire from the back of the work to the front of the work through the next hole in the metal. Come up through the loop left behind in Step 2. Pass the end of the wire back through the hole you just came through until a loop the same size as the first remains on the front of your work. Again, press the loop flat against the sheet metal.

4 Continue repeating Steps 2 and 3 until your chain stitches reach your desired length. Anchor the last stitch by tacking it down with the wire tail, travel through the final hole, passing over the top of the final loop, and go back through the final hole. Anchor your wire tail to the back of your work.

COVER IT UP

Sadly, embroidered projects aren't nearly as pretty on the back side as they are on the front. How you will conceal the wrong side of the work is an important thing to keep in mind. A second piece of metal can act as a cover. Ribbon and fabric accents are another option.

Whipstitch

1 For this stitch, use punch pliers to create a series of holes ¼" (6 mm) apart and ⅛" (2 mm) from the edge of a length of sheet metal.

2 Anchor the end of a 24" (61 cm) piece of wire to the back side of your work.

3 Bring your wire from the back of your work to the front wrapping it over the edge of the metal. Pass the wire through the next hole in line and through to the back of the work.

4 Continue working from front to back wrapping the edge along the entire length of the metal. Anchor the tail of wire to the back of the work.

Blanket Stitch

This stitch is created in the same ways as a whipstitch with one small change. So, repeat Steps 1 through 3 of Whipstitch (above). Then:

1 After bringing the wire from the back of the work through to the front for the next stitch, go through the wrapping on the edge of the previous stitch. Then pass your wire through to the back of the work.

2 Continue to repeat Steps 1 and 2 until you reach the end of your work. Anchor the tail of wire to the back of your work.

EXPLORING
rustic color

One of the most frustrating things for jewelry makers can be when they discover they have fallen into a color rut. They find themselves always working in the same palette of colors and longing to do something different. Where does one begin? Creating with color can be as intimidating for some as it is fun for others. But, it is possible to create color combinations that have a rustic feel, while still being creative and modern.

The secret to beautiful assemblages of beads, metal, and wire that are both colorful and expressive is simple. Every piece of jewelry you create is an opportunity to tell a story. So, take a moment to think about what you want to say. The things you intend to express can set you up with everything you need to create a beautiful color combination. Look to that intention for the inspiration you need.

SEASONS

The earth has a wealth of inspiration to offer in the form of the changing seasons.

WINTER: dark blues, grays, crisp whites make layers of woolen knits and rosy cheeks pop

SPRING: pastel florals, combined with the brown colors of the soil they bloom from

SUMMER: deep reds, fiery oranges, against a blazing yellow sky that crackles paint

PLACES

The places you travel, literally or imaginatively, can be places for color refuge.

FOREST FLOORS: deep brown, emerald greens, taupe and tan, deep honey yellow

BIG CITIES: midnight blue, against metallic gray, and hints of amber glow

MUSEUMS: a little of everything grounded in the history of art

ELEMENTS

These constants that help sustain our lives can help sustain our color creativity.

AIR: the gathering tones of a pending storm or the briskness of swift-moving clouds

WATER: crashing waves in the cold of Maine or the serenity along a coastal beach

FIRE: creating warmth near our hearth or memories at our campsite

EMOTIONS

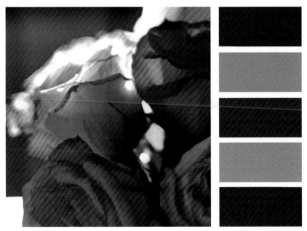

Looking to your heart and how you feel at any moment can be another color-drenched muse.

JOY: bright pink and baby blue with a weathered heather

PASSION: blood red rolled up in heart-pumping purple against industrial black

SORROW: somber bits of blue under a yellow umbrella on a lonely city street

The phrase "the possibilities are endless" is one I use a lot, and granted, it is a bit cliché. But really, I just can't get enough of color, and the ways to combine color are infinite. Sometimes the way I choose to put colors together comes by complete chance, but more often than not, I find I need to seek inspiration. I am always delighted to share what works for me, and I encourage you to explore these associations to find what works for you.

The way you talk about a color combination can really impact the impression it leaves when working on a product listing or even telling a friend about it over the phone. For example, if I say, "I made a blue and yellow bracelet," it might sound like I made something to cheer on my son's football team. Now, if I talk about the combination in a way that is more expressive, you'll see it in a completely different light. "I created a bracelet with crisp lake water blues, delicate buttercup yellow, and it has deep oxidized brass accents that remind me of the time we visited my aunt's cottage in the mountains." Words have visual power!

Many artists devote entire sketchbooks to things that inspire them. Jewelry artists should, too! Try creating a splash page of colors and images that speak to you. Cut pictures from magazines, print images from your favorite blogs, or save art cards from a visit to your local museum. I think you'll find it not only a cathartic activity but an oh-so-wonderful treasure to turn to on a day when you lack inspiration.

STAY GROUNDED

One of the things that sets rustic color combinations apart from the rest is that each is grounded in a deep base color: black or brown. The shadows that the deeper tones create give your designs depth and the appearance of age—quite literally, as if they have been unearthed from the ground.

TECHNIQUES

Coiling

Spiraling

Patina

TOOLS

Round-nose pliers

Chain-nose pliers

Wire cutters

Coiling Gizmo

Liver of sulfur

Polishing cloth

Steel wool

Micro torch

Dish of water

Bracelet mandrel

Wax

MATERIALS

18" (45.5 cm) 16-gauge annealed steel wire

5' (1.5 m) 20-gauge sterling silver dead-soft wire

6" (15 cm) 20-gauge copper wire

Five lampwork-glass rings

Lampwork beads by Yee Kwan

Finshed size: 8" (20.5 cm)

among anemone
EARRINGS

Fine silver droplets float to the surface of these lampwork-glass rings like bubbles to the surface of water. The bubbling source is unknown when hidden in the arms of an anemone. As you find this on your arm, you'll catch yourself spinning the rings and sliding the tiny links along the band. Each one is uniquely colored and as enchanting as the life in a coral reef.

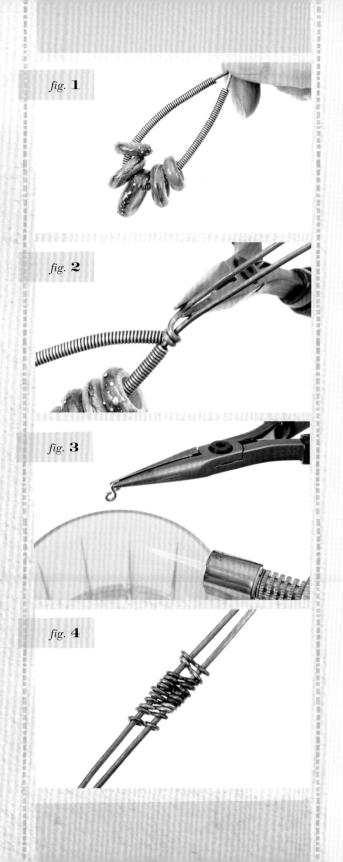

fig. **1**

fig. **2**

fig. **3**

fig. **4**

1 First, create the sterling wire coil that clusters all the lampwork rings together. Use the Coiling Gizmo and 20-gauge sterling silver wire to make a 5″ (12.5 cm) coil. Trim ends. Oxidize with liver of sulfur (see page 26) to create your patina.

2 Center the sterling coil on an 18″ (45.5 cm) piece of steel wire that has been cleaned. Form a U-shaped bend in the steel and add the five lampwork beads so they rest in the bend of the U. (**Figure 1**)

3 Wrap one length of the steel wire around the other as if closing a large wrapped loop. Do not trim the excess wire. Use chain-nose pliers to bend the wrapped wire in a way that makes it run alongside the other wire. (**Figure 2**)

4 With round-nose pliers, make twelve small figure-eight links from ½″ (1.3 cm) pieces of 20-gauge copper wire.

5 Hold each figure-eight link in the flame of the micro torch until a slight red glow appears and then quickly quench in water. Repeat for each figure-eight link. Vary the time the link is in the heat of the flame to get a variety of colors pulled to the surface of the metal. Set aside. (**Figure 3**)

6 Dry the figure-eight links and slide them onto the parallel wires of the bangle. (**Figure 4**)

7   About 5" (12.5 cm) from the spot where the steel wire is wrapped to trap the figure-eight links onto the bangle, hold the steel wires side by side with chain-nose pliers and wrap one wire around the other as before (**Figure 5**). Trim excess wire to 2" (5 cm) and use the round-nose pliers to form a closed spiral. This will act as the hook of your clasp (**Figure 6**).

8   Trim the remaining length of the steel wire to 2" (5 cm) and form a second closed spiral. (**Figure 7**)

9   Form the bangle around a bracelet mandrel to achieve the oval shape for your wrist. The spiral hook should easily slip into the U of the coil and close the bangle when worn. (**Figure 8**)

10 Seal all exposed steel with wax to prevent rusting.

REMEMBER, IT RUSTS

Steel is a fantastic medium to work with, but it is important to remember that it will rust if left unsealed. Taking just a few moments to rub wax onto the surface of the metal will give it a much longer wearable life. If you find that rust has started to form at any time, buff the area with steel wool and coat again with wax.

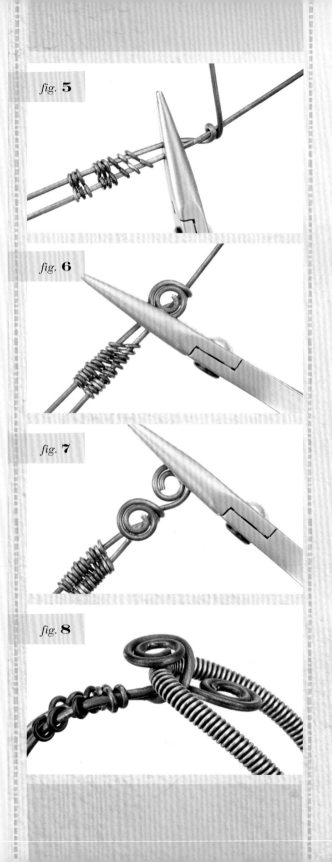

fig. **5**

fig. **6**

fig. **7**

fig. **8**

TECHNIQUES

Patina

Coiling

Ear wires

TOOLS

Round-nose pliers

Chain-nose pliers

Punch pliers

Liver of sulfur

Polishing cloth

Chasing hammer

Bench block

Alcohol ink (color shown: pearl)

Craft mat

Sealant

Paintbrush

MATERIALS

12" (30.5 cm) 20-gauge oxidized sterling silver dead-soft wire

12" (30.5 cm) 20-gauge anodized copper wire (color shown: vintage bronze)

Two 34 mm brass eight-petal flowers

Two 19 mm brass six-petal flowers

Two lampwork-glass head pins

Lampwork beads by Kerry Bogert

Finished size: 2½" (6.5 cm)

blooming twine
EARRINGS

Arboretum walks on winter days warm your soul with memories of summer's blooms. As if captured in ice, pearlized components are shadowed by tooled and textured pieces of the past. Each swings lightly from the ear and holds with it an afternoon breeze under an unbelievably blue sky.

1   Lay out the brass flower components on the craft mat. Use the alcohol ink patina technique (see page 31) to apply pearl color to the two smaller flowers.

2   While the inks dry on the small flowers, use the chasing hammer and bench block to tool the surface of both of the larger flower components (**Figure 1**). Buff the large flowers with a polishing cloth to highlight the texture.

3   Use the punch pliers to add a single hole to one petal on each flower (**Figure 2**). Slide a head pin through the punch hole and use chain-nose pliers to spiral the head-pin wire (**Figure 3**). Bend the spiral so it sits flat against the back of the brass flower. Repeat this step with the other flower and head pin. Set aside.

4   When the ink patina has completely dried, seal the small flowers with sealant and let dry. Set aside.

5   Cut two 6" (15 cm) pieces of 20-gauge sterling silver wire. Oxidize the wire with liver of sulfur (see page 26). Then polish back the oxidation with a polishing cloth.

6   Form a small open spiral at one end of one piece of wire. Set aside.

7   Using round-nose pliers, make a small coil of 20-gauge anodized copper wire. Trim to four wraps of coil. Make two. Set aside.

fig. **1**

fig. **2**

fig. **3**

fig. **4**

fig. **5**

PRE-OXIDIZING WIRE

Do you find that you rarely use your sterling wire in its shiny form? Are you always oxidizing it? Well, that is a step for most projects that you can do in advance. Oxidize several feet of wire at a time, store it already blackened, and have it ready to use in finished projects.

8   Assemble the pieces (**Figure 4**). Slide the beaded flower component, the small coil of anodized wire, and the patina flower component onto one piece of spiraled 20-gauge sterling wire.

9   Form a loop with the sterling wire that is large enough for the brass components to spin inside the earring. With chasing hammer and bench block, flatten the loop of wire formed, while carefully holding the flower components out of the way. Use a short length of 20-gauge anodized copper wire to secure the loop. Trim excess copper wire; do not trim the sterling wire.

10 With the remaining sterling silver wire, form the ear wire for the earring using round-nose pliers. (**Figure 5**)

11 Hammer the arch of the ear wire with the chasing hammer and bench block. Again, be sure to hold the components out of the path of the hammer to keep them from being damaged.

12 Repeat Steps 6–11 for the second earring.

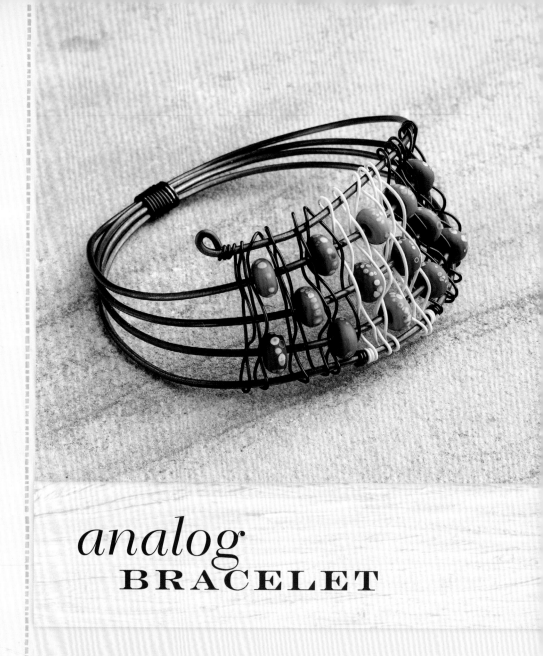

TECHNIQUES

Simple loops

Wire embroidery

TOOLS

Bracelet mandrel

Round-nose pliers

Wire cutters

Steel wool

MATERIALS

3' (91.5 cm) 16-gauge annealed steel wire

18" (45.5 cm) 20-gauge colored copper wire (color shown: ivory [turquoise in step shots])

3' (91.5 cm) 22-gauge colored copper wire (color shown: purple [teal in step shots])

Fourteen 6mm petite lampwork-glass rondelles

Lampwork beads by Mika Collins

Finshed size: 7½" (19 cm)

analog
BRACELET

Woven among satellites' digital signals are ghosts of analog messages, each little blip and beep a connection to a yesteryear when love letters were written with pen and paper and veterans remembered Morse code. This cuff-style bangle is wrapped in those linear links to lost liaisons.

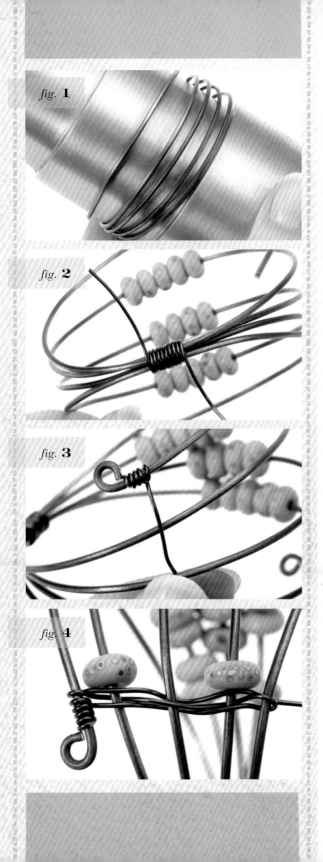

fig. **1**

fig. **2**

fig. **3**

fig **4**

1   Set to work creating this bangle by preparing the steel wire for use in the project. Using the steel wool, clean the carbon coating on the surface of the wire off of a 3' (91.5 cm) length.

2   Wrap the cleaned steel around a bracelet mandrel five times on an area of the mandrel one size smaller than your finished size. (The wire will expand when removed from the mandrel.) Remove the wrapped wire from the mandrel. You should have two tails of wire on either side of three center lengths of wire. (**Figure 1**)

3   Slip the fourteen lampwork-glass beads onto the steel wire and arrange them in a way that moves five beads onto the first wrap of the wire, four on the middle wrap, and the five remaining onto the last wrap of wire. This becomes the front of your bangle.

4   Using a 12" (30.5 cm) length of 22-gauge colored copper wire, secure the back side of the bangle by pinching together the steel wire and tightly wrapping it with the colored wire. Trim the ends of the copper wire and tuck against the steel. (**Figure 2**)

5   Arrange the steel wire so that the wire flares from the back where it is secured out to the front focal area. Then, use round-nose pliers to form a simple loop at each end of the tails of steel wire.

6   Secure a 15" (38 cm) piece of 22-gauge colored copper wire to the left side of the bangle front near the simple loop of steel wire by wrapping the copper wire to the steel. Make sure that all the beads are moved to the right and out of the way of your wrapping. (**Figure 3**)

7   Begin to weave the copper wire in an over-under pattern working back and forth three times. Then, slide the first lampwork beads on the top and bottom rows over against the woven wire. (**Figure 4**)

8   Continue weaving the wire in an over-under pattern, working back and forth three times. Then slide the first bead in the center row over against the wrapping. (**Figure 5**)

9   Continue weaving in pattern, working from left to right across the bangle and creating a grid of beads among the woven wire. In the center area, secure the copper wire, trim the end, and start again with another length of 20-gauge copper wire in a contrasting color. After working the center beads into the pattern, secure the second wire to the steel and begin again with a new piece of copper, going back to the first color.

10 Once you have reached the right side of the bangle and all the beads have been worked into the pattern, finish weaving four rows of wire in the over-under pattern back and forth three times. Secure the tail of wire to the steel wire near the simple loop on the right side. Trim excess wire. (**Figure 6**)

11 To prevent rusting, seal the steel wire with wax.

ON PERFECTION

Some designs call for really tight, crisp, uniform wirework. Others can be much more relaxed and free flowing. Analog is a project that allows itself to be a little on the imperfect side. There is movement in layers of wire being woven together and, try as you might, the wraps just aren't going to be perfect. So, exaggerate that and make the inconsistencies work throughout the piece. Embrace its imperfections and love it anyway.

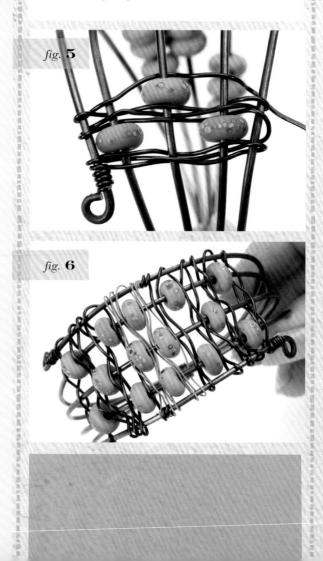

fig. **5**

fig. **6**

aurora
NECKLACE

AURORA NECKLACE •

47

TECHNIQUES

Patina

Wrapped loops

Clasps

TOOLS

Round-nose pliers

Chain-nose pliers

Wire cutters

Disc cutter

Round needle-nose file

Hammer

Punch pliers

Dapping set

Micro torch

Fire brick

Sealant

MATERIALS

30-gauge sheet metal copper

18" (45.5 cm) 16-gauge copper wire

14" (35.5 cm) length of 3.5mm brass rolo chain

4mm round metal spacer beads

Five 18–20mm small lampwork-glass hollow beads

Lampwork beads by Kerry Bogert

Finished size: 16" (40.5 cm)

Named for the Roman goddess of dawn, Aurora, this piece features early hour hues of warm amber and honey yellow, brought to life on the surface of the hand-forged metal discs. Each disc acts as an echo to the golden hollow glass beads, and the finished piece takes on an antique quality. This wears high on the neck and would have been paired perfectly with stola dresses of ancient Rome.

1   Set off building this necklace by cutting the gradu-
    ated discs that will frame each of the lampwork
    beads in this design. Cut two ⅞" (2.2 cm), six ¾"
    (2 cm), eight ⅝" (1.5 cm), eight ½" (1.3 cm), and four
    ⅜" (1 cm) for a total of thirty discs. (**Figure 1**)

2   With punch pliers, make a hole in the center of each
    disc. Then, with the dapping set, cup each disc.

3   Lay out the cupped discs on the fire brick and heat
    each one with the micro torch until a pale purple
    color comes to the surface of the metal. Allow to
    cool completely. (**Figure 2**)

4   Once the discs have cooled, spray the outside of the
    discs with sealant and allow the protective finish to
    dry. Set aside.

5   With round-nose pliers, make a wrapped loop at one
    end of a 15" (38 cm) piece of 16-gauge wire. Slide
    the disc beads, spacer beads, and lampwork beads
    onto the wire, up against the wrapped loop, in the
    following order: ⅜" disc, spacer, ½" disc, spacer, ⅝"
    disc, spacer, lampwork bead, spacer, ⅝" disc, spacer,
    ½" disc, spacer, ⅜" disc, spacer, ½" disc, spacer, ⅝"
    disc, spacer, ¾" disc, spacer, lampwork bead, spacer,
    ¾" disc, spacer, ⅝" disc, spacer, ½" disc, spacer,
    ⅝" disc, spacer, ¾" disc, spacer, ⅞" disc, spacer,
    lampwork bead. At this point, you have reached the
    center front of the necklace. (**Figure 3**)

fig. **1**

fig. **2**

fig. **3**

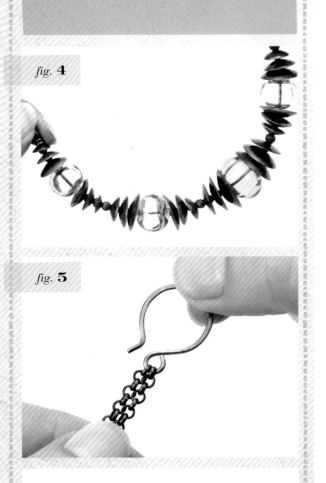

fig. **4**

fig. **5**

6   Work the pattern as a mirror image to match the side just strung.

7   On the other side, create a second wrapped loop with the remaining copper wire to lock the beads in place. Trim excess wire. Then, form the beaded wire into an arch to follow the curve of your neckline. (**Figure 4**)

8   Cut a piece of rolo chain to 14″ (35.5 cm) in length. Thread one end of chain through the wrapped loop at one end of the beaded wire, essentially folding the chain in half. Set aside.

9   Using a 3″ (7.5 cm) piece of 16-gauge copper wire, make a basic hook clasp with a simple loop at one end.

10   Open the simple loop of the clasp with chain-nose pliers and connect the two ends of rolo chain together. Close the loop (**Figure 5**). The free loop of your beaded wire will act as the catch for your clasp.

A HOLE IN (MORE THAN) ONE

When making these cupped discs, you need to punch the holes in the center before shaping them; the punch pliers aren't shaped in a way to accommodate the doming. At the same time, though, when you shape the discs in the dapping tool, the small punched hole can lose its round shape. What to do? Simply use the tip of a round-nose needle file to round the hole back out. It just takes a few twists of the file, and you are ready to string the discs.

TECHNIQUES

Simple loops

Wrapped loops

Coiling

Ear wires

Patina

TOOLS

Ring mandrel

Round-nose pliers

Chain-nose pliers

Wire cutters

Chasing hammer

Nylon mallet

Bench block

Liver of sulfur

Polishing cloth

Rotary tumbler

MATERIALS

12' (3.6 m) 24-gauge sterling silver wire

18" (45.5 cm) 18-gauge sterling silver wire

8" (20.5 cm) 16-gauge stainless steel wire

4 lampwork-glass lollipop-shaped head pins

Lampwork glass beads by Kerry Bogert

Finshed size: 3½" (9 cm)

candy chandelier
EARRINGS

These earrings have a sassy youthfulness to them that makes me think of heart flutters that happen when your sweetheart approaches. The crushed-glass-covered head pins add a hint of playful color but could easily be swapped out for a color that makes you swoon.

fig. **1**

HEAD OF THE GLASS

More and more glass artists are starting to make lampwork-glass head pins available to eager beaders. The wire the glass is attached to can usually be found in sterling, brass, or steel. As for the glass itself, there are so many shapes, sizes, and colors to choose from. Just search "lampwork head pins" on Etsy.com to start exploring your options.

1 Begin this design by prepping the head pins to become dangles. Trim the long wire ends of the four head pins to ½" (1.3 cm) and use round-nose pliers to form a simple loop on each head pin. Two will be parallel to the flat area of the head pin; the other two will be oriented perpendicular to the flat area. Set aside.

2 Next you'll create the outer coiled component in this earring. Tightly coil a 4' (122 cm) length of 24-gauge sterling silver wire around a 5" (12.5 cm) piece of 20-gauge sterling silver. Once 4" (10 cm) of the core wire has been coiled, trim the excess coiling wire from each end. Center the coil on the core wire and use round-nose pliers to make a simple loop with the exposed wire at each end of the coil. Make two.

3 Take the piece just created and working from the center out, wrap the coil around a ring mandrel at the size 10 mark. Do not form a complete ring; allow the ends to remain straight, nearly meeting. Repeat for the other piece. Set aside.

4 Flush cut and file the ends of two pieces of 16-gauge steel wire that are 4" (10 cm). Mold the center of the wire around the ring mandrel at the size 8 mark. Let both ends of the wire splay straight; don't form a complete circle. With round-nose pliers, form a loop at one end of the wire that bends in toward the center of the link and form a loop with the other end that rolls out (**Figure 1**). Make two.

5 With fine steel wool, clean the carbon off the surface of the steel wire. Then seal with finishing wax. Set aside.

6 Using liver of sulfur, oxidize the head pins, sterling links from Step 3, and two 4" (10 cm) pieces of 20-gauge sterling silver (see page 26). Rinse and polish with a polishing cloth.

7 Open the loops of the glass head-pin dangles and attach one to each of the four components created in the previous steps.

8 Using one of the pre-oxidized pieces of 20-gauge sterling, start to form a wrapped loop with round-nose pliers about 1.5" (3.8 mm) from one end. Before closing the loop, take one of the steel components and slip it between the simple loops of one of the sterling components. Slip this new large link onto the wrapped loop and close the loop. Trim excess wire and file smooth. Repeat for the second earring. **(Figure 2)**

9 Form a fishhook ear wire with the straight wire remaining after the wrapped loop. Hammer the arch of the hook with the chasing hammer.

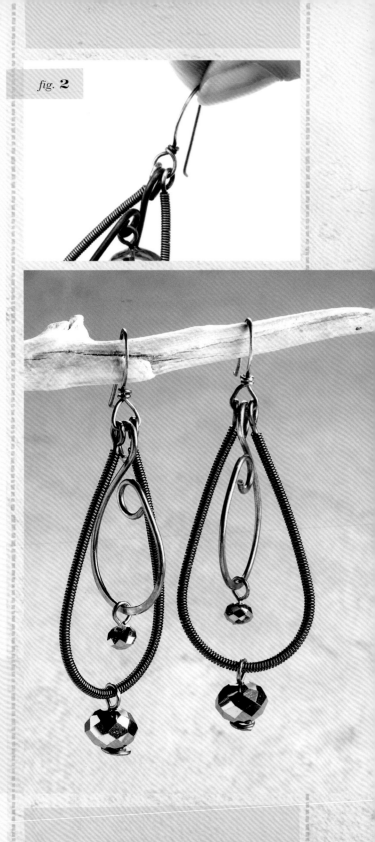

fig. **2**

alternate view

These earrings were made using the same method but utilize all brass wire and blue-colored copper wire. Czech fire-polished glass crystals and handmade head pins act as the dangles.

TECHNIQUES

Chunky wrapped loops

Coiling

Patina

TOOLS

Chain-nose pliers

Round-nose pliers

Wire cutters

¼" (6 mm) mandrel

Liver of sulfur

Polishing cloth

Rotary tumbler

MATERIALS

12" (30.5 cm) 16-gauge sterling silver wire

18" (45.5 cm) 16-gauge copper wire

3.5' (106 cm) 18-gauge sterling silver wire

Five 8mm lampwork-glass rondelles

Lampwork beads by J. C. Herrell

Finshed size: 8" (20.5 cm), expandable to larger sizes

sprockets in pockets
BRACELET

The modern age of cell phones and laptops owes its beginnings to the industrial age of springs and sprockets. With this sturdy, versatile bracelet, pay homage to cars with wooden tires and a time when an operator connected your phone call.

1 With round-nose pliers and 18-gauge sterling silver wire, make chunky wrapped loops on either side of the five lampwork rondelle beads.

2 Coil a 12″ (31.5 cm) piece of 16-gauge copper wire around the ¼″ (6 mm) mandrel. Leave a tail at one end that is about 2″ (5 cm) long.

3 Coil an 18″ (45.5 cm) piece of 16-gauge sterling wire around the ¼″ (6 mm) mandrel.

4 Slightly spread the copper coil apart. With wire cutters, cut off a section of coil that is six wraps long from the side with the 2″ (5 cm) tail. Then cut a second six-wrap piece from the remaining coil. (**Figure 1**)

5 Cut three six-wrap coil sections from the sterling wire coil.

6 With chain-nose pliers, grab the last wrap on one of the coil pieces and pull it up 90 degree so that it sits perpendicular to the rest of the coils. Repeat on the other side of the coil (**Figure 2**). Then, repeat on the other three links that do not have the tail of wire.

7 The piece of coil with the tail of wire is going to become the hook side of the clasp in your finished bracelet. To form the hook, use chain-nose pliers to form a 45-degree bend in the wire where the straight tail meets the coil. Next, wrap that bent wire around the larger end of your round-nose pliers. Trim excess wire so that there is only a slight gap between the hook and the coil. (**Figure 3**)

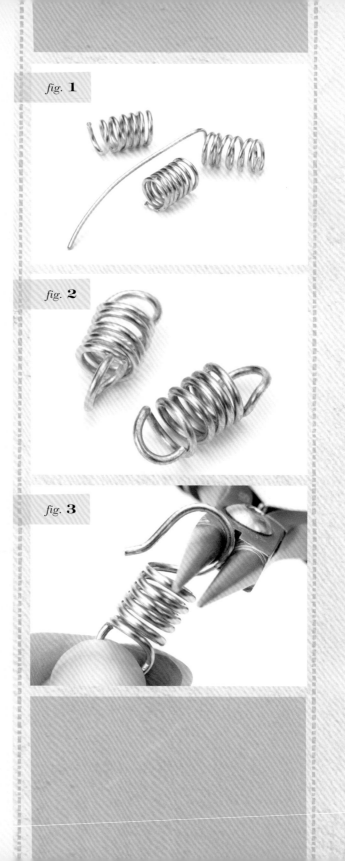

fig. **1**

fig. **2**

fig. **3**

fig. **4**

fig. **5**

ADJUSTABLE LINKS

This design is very versatile because it can be easily sized to fit larger wrists. Simply open up the coils a little more to get more length. To adjust it smaller, cut the coils to four or five wraps long.

8 With chain-nose pliers, open one side of a coil piece as you would a jump ring. Attach it to one of the chunky wrapped loops of the beaded links. Close the coil (**Figure 4**). Repeat this step mixing up the copper and sterling coil links between the beaded links. End with the clasp coil link (**Figure 5**).

TIP: It is important to make sure that the coil is closed all the way so links won't be lost when wearing the bracelet. Work the arch back and forth as you would a jump ring, until it is fully closed.

9 Using liver of sulfur, oxidize the linked bracelet (see page 26). Then use a polishing cloth to buff back the tarnish.

10 Tumble in a rotary tumbler to work-harden links and finish polishing.

TECHNIQUES

Patina

Embroidery

Metal cutting

Riveting

Jump rings

Clasps

TOOLS

Round-nose pliers

Chain-nose pliers

Wire cutters

Metal snips

Files

Riveting tool

Punch pliers

Sawdust

Vinegar

Resealable container

Liver of sulfur

Paintbrush

Sealant

Superglue

MATERIALS

10" (25.5 cm) 18-gauge copper wire

2' (61 cm) 20-gauge colored copper wire (color shown: amber)

30-gauge copper sheet metal

16" (41 cm) length of brass rolo chain

1 lampwork-glass head pin

Rivets

Lampwork beads by Kerry Bogert

Finshed size: 3" (7.5 cm) pendant, total length 20" (51 cm)

chrysanthemum
PENDANT

As the fall treescape changes to sirens of yellow, orange, and red, at the ground level, chrysanthemums come into bloom. Hundreds of petals cluster close together before unfurling into an explosion of color. This rustic mum preserves in sculptural form a single blossom from one of those prolific plants.

fig. 1

fig. 2

fig. 3

1   Transfer the chrysanthemum illustration provided on page 58 to the surface of a 3″ (7.5 cm) piece of 30-gauge copper sheet metal. Use the metal snips to cut out the outer petal edge of the design. Transfer the two petal shapes as well. Cut six of each size petal for a total of twelve petals. (**Figure 1**)

2   Use a file to round over the tips of the petals into a smooth arch.

3   With the punch pliers, punch holes into the metal base as shown, creating an inside circle of six punches and outside circle of twelve punches. Punch the petal pieces as shown. (**Figure 2**)

4   Following the instructions on page 29, use the sawdust and vinegar in a resealable container to patina all the copper pieces. Allow time for the patina to develop.

5   While waiting for the patina to form, take a few moments to create two jump rings from 18-gauge copper wire, a simple hook clasp (see page 21), and a small figure-eight link with your round-nose pliers. Oxidize with liver of sulfur and set aside.

6   Once the patina is fully developed on the surface of the metal, remove all the components from the sawdust mixture and allow to air dry. With a soft bristled brush, wipe away any wood fibers still on the surface of the metal. Seal the patina with spray sealant and allow sealant to completely dry.

7   With the riveting tool, connect metal petals via the inside ring of six holes in the metal base. Every other hole will have a single large petal; the others will have a single large petal and two small petals. (**Figure 3**)

TIP: Detailed instructions are provided with this riveting tool as well as the small rivets used. This is a really handy tool to have in the studio for making these simple cold connections.

8   With round-nose pliers, very gently shape the metal petals to appear slightly curled. This adds wonderful depth to the finished look of the flower. (**Figure 4**)

9   Secure a 24" (61 cm) piece of 20-gauge colored copper wire to the flower base, tucking it between the two layers of petals. Loop the wire in and out of the holes between the layers of petals, working alternately on the face of the flower and in the back, for a total of twelve wire loops around the outside edge (**Figure 5**). Secure the wire tail between the two layers of petals.

fig. **4**

fig. **5**

fig. **6**

TO MATCH OR NOT TO MATCH

Many beginner beaders really love to make matched sets of jewelry where the earrings match the bracelet that matches the necklace. Oftentimes, more experienced beaders will shy away from that, wanting each piece to be unique. I like to take an approach that falls between those two. Meaning, I like things to coordinate, but not necessarily look like a matched set. Chrysanthemum and Blooming Twine are two projects that illustration my point. They use the same beads, have similar floral themes, and would look lovely worn together, but they stand just as strong on their own as individual pieces.

10 Taking a second piece of colored copper wire, use the same technique to create an inner ring of wire petals through the remaining holes in the center of the base flower. Secure the tail and trim excess wire. (**Figure 6**)

11 Trim the wire off a lampwork-glass head pin with wire cutters and use superglue to adhere the glass head of the head pin to the center of the flower pendant.

12 With chain-nose pliers, open one of the jump rings created in Step 5 and attach it to one of the outer two holes in the flower pendant and an 8″ (20.5 cm) length of rolo brass chain. Do the same with the second jump ring and a second length of chain.

13 Finish by attaching the wire clasp components to the last links in the chain.

TECHNIQUES

Jump rings

Wrapped loops

Simple loops

TOOLS

Round-nose pliers

Chain-nose pliers

Wire cutters

¼" (6 mm) mandrel

Ring mandrel

Chasing hammer

Bench block

Liver of sulfur

Polishing cloth

MATERIALS

4' (1.2 m) 16-gauge copper wire

6.5' (2 m) 18-gauge copper wire

Eleven 40–45mm extra-large hollow lampwork-glass beads

1 g size 11° glass seed beads

12" (30.5 cm) length of copper chain

Lampwork beads by Aja Vaz

Finished size: 32" (81.5 cm)

moroccan archways
NECKLACE

I often find myself in complete awe of ancient architecture. I marvel at the thought of how such beautiful things could be formed with the most primitive of tools. Every country has its own unique style of historic architecture, and this necklace was inspired by ornate archways seen in the streets of Morocco. Though I have never been there, this piece acts a reminder of the beauty waiting to be visited.

1 Begin this necklace by creating the links that feature the archway-style links that mimic the patterns in the glass beads. Cut six 8" (20.5 cm) lengths of 16-gauge copper wire.

2 About 3" (7.5 cm) from an end of an 8" (20.3 cm) piece of wire, form a bend in the wire. Bring the wire into a position that has the two lengths running parallel to each other. Then, splay the wires apart about ¼" (6 mm) from the bend. (**Figure 1**) Grip the area of wire that should remain parallel with chain-nose pliers to help hold them together.

3 Wrap the splayed lengths of wire around the smallest end of the ring mandrel (**Figure 2**). Wrap the shorter end around the longer as if closing a wrapped loop (**Figure 3**). Trim excess wire after wrapping. Repeat for all six pieces of 16-gauge wire.

4 Use the chasing hammer and bench block to flatten the archway-shaped links. Repeat for all six archway links.

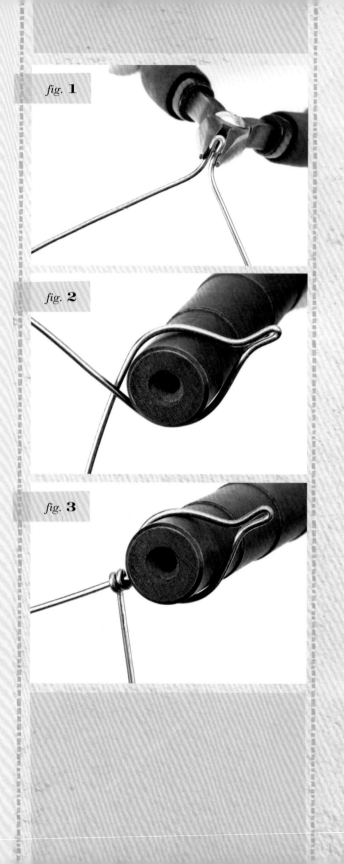

fig. **1**

fig. **2**

fig. **3**

fig. **4**

fig. **5**

5 Slide one hollow lampwork bead onto an archway link. Trim excess wire to about ⅜" (1 cm) and use chain-nose pliers to form a simple loop. (**Figure 4**) Repeat for all six archway links.

6 With 18-gauge copper wire, create three beaded links with wrapped loops at either end from three of the remaining lampwork hollow beads.

7 Again using the 18-gauge copper wire, create two beaded links with simple loops at each end from the final two lampwork hollow beads.

8 Open the simple loop at one end of an archway link with chain-nose pliers and connect it to the wrapped loop end of one beaded link. Close the loop. Add a second archway link to the opposite side of the beaded link in the same manner. Repeat this with the other wrapped-loop beaded links and archway links to make a total of three longer links. (**Figure 5**)

9 Open the simple loop at one end of a remaining beaded link with chain-nose pliers and connect it to the point on one of the archway links. Close the simple loops. Repeat on the other side of the beaded link, connecting to the archway loop of another larger link. Repeat for the final beaded link that connects the last of the archway links together. Set aside.

10 Using 18-gauge copper wire, create a coil of at least sixty wraps around the ¼" (6 mm) steel mandrel. Use the technique described on page 20 to create sixty jump rings.

11 Attach ten jump rings to each of the archway links in the necklace. Before closing the jump ring, add a single seed bead to each ring. Repeat this step until all sixty jump rings have been attached to the archway links. (**Figure 6**)

12 Oxidize the beaded portion of the necklace in a liver of sulfur and warm-water solution. Copper oxidizes very quickly in warm LOS, so you needn't do more than dip it in the liquid. Use a polishing cloth to highlight the wirework and remove the tarnish.

13 Open one of the seed-beaded jump rings at one end of the beaded portion of the necklace and attach it to a 12" (30.5 cm) length of premade copper chain. Do the same at the opposite end of the beaded portion, attaching it to the other end of the copper chain. (**Figure 7**)

TIP: Thanks to the long finished length of this necklace, no clasp is needed. It easily slips over your head.

fig. **6**

fig. **7**

BIG BEADS

Working with large beads can sometimes be intimidating, but I find the longer the finished necklace, the more proportionate the beads become. This necklace is an example of just that. On their own, these beads measure as large as 35mm across, which is quite big for a glass bead. The extra-long 32" (81.3 cm) length of this design balances the scale of the beads and looks beautiful, not bulky, when worn.

mountain bride
NECKLACE

TECHNIQUES

Coiling

Jump rings

Wrapped loops

Simple loops

Clasps

Patina

TOOLS

Round-nose pliers

Chain-nose pliers

Wire cutters

¼" (6 mm) mandrel

Coiling tool

Chasing hammer

Bench block

Polishing cloth

Ammonia

Cotton balls

Resealable bag

Alcohol ink (color shown: cranberry)

Craft mat

Sealant

Paintbrush

MATERIALS

10' (3 m) 16g brass wire

14' (4.25 m) 20g brass wire

18–20 clear glass head pins

Lampwork beads by Anne Lichtenstine

Finshed size: 18" (45.5 cm)

Special occasions often spark the creating of a future heirloom that will be passed down for generations. Wrapped in the warmth of love, this baroque-inspired design has all the drama of velvet drapes and the softness of snow-capped mountains. Although this piece was created in a modern studio, the style gives it a feeling of age and history.

1 Begin this necklace by creating the jump rings that will be used to connect all the elements of the finished piece together. Coil a piece of 16-gauge brass around the ¼" (6 mm) steel mandrel until you have at least thirty wraps. Use the technique described on page 20 to cut the coil into jump rings. Set aside.

2 Next, create the thirty-two figure-eight links used to build the chain that the focal area hangs from. Cut thirty-two pieces of 16-gauge wire to 1¼" (2 cm) lengths. Use round nose pliers to create a simple loop on each end of the wire, making the figure eight (**Figure 1**). Repeat for all pieces.

3 With chain-nose pliers, open jump rings to connect figure-eight links into a chain. Lay the figure-eight links side by side and connect the ends with a single jump ring (**Figure 2**). Create two lengths of chain that are each sixteen figure-eight links long and connected with seven jump rings per length of chain. (One length of chain will have an eighth jump ring at the end that will later act as the loop for the clasp.) Set aside.

4 Using the same technique shown in Step 2, create three smaller figure-eight links from a ½" (1.3 cm) piece of 16-gauge brass wire. These links will be used for the center pendant. Use chain-nose pliers to open the loops of the links and connect them into a chain. Set aside. (**Figure 3**)

5 Create the dangles that will act as the pendant and accents from the glass head pins. Use round-nose pliers to form wrapped loops with the straight length of wire protruding from the glass head (**Figure 4**). Any excess wire can be used to add an extra layer of wrapping to the loops for a chunkier style wrapped loop. Mix things up and add additional visual interest by making some of the head pins have simple loops instead of wrapped loops.

6 Connect the dangles just created to jump rings created in Step 1 as follows. Open a jump ring, add one dangle, and close the jump ring. Repeat for a second single dangle. Open a jump ring, add two dangles, and close the jump ring. Repeat for a second double dangle. Set aside.

fig. **1**

fig. **2**

fig. **3**

fig. **4**

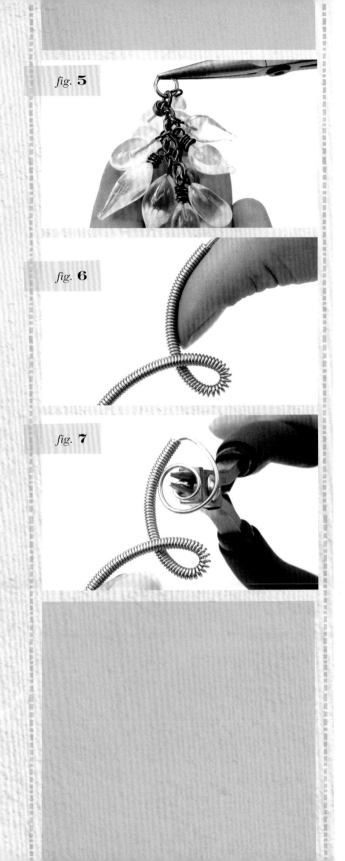

fig. **5**

fig. **6**

fig. **7**

7 To construct the pendant of dangles, open the loops of the trio of figure-eight links from Step 4, one at a time, adding dangles, then closing the links. When you have added the remaining dangles and have reached the last link in the trio chain, attach a single jump ring to the end. Set aside. (**Figure 5**)

8 Now we'll create the coiled swirls that are the main focus of this design. Start with the main coil that is in the front center of the finished piece. Using the Coiling Gizmo and 20-gauge brass wire, make a 3½" (9 cm) coil. Trim ends flush.

9 Slide the brass coil onto the center of a 10" (25.5 cm) piece of 16-gauge brass wire. Cross the ends of the core wire past each other to form a loop in the coil. Use your thumbs to add a slight arch to either side of the coils that flow from the center loop. (**Figure 6**)

10 With wire cutters, trim the exposed core wire so that each side is of equal length (about 3" [7.6 cm]). Use round-nose pliers to make open spirals that twist in toward the center loop. (**Figure 7**)

11 Flatten the outer edges of spiral with the flat end of the chasing hammer and bench block. Be careful not to strike your coil. Set aside.

TIP: You may want to set your tools aside and do a little handwork to finesse the look of this link.

12 Create the next coiled link in the series. Tightly coil a 2¾" (7 cm) area of an 8" (20.5 cm) piece of 16-gauge brass with 20-gauge brass. Trim excess 20-gauge wire being sure not to cut the inner core wire. Then, trim the core wire so that there are equal lengths of core wire exposed at each end of the coil.

TIP: Why tightly coil this link instead of using the Coiling Gizmo? A tighter coil will appear smaller than the Gizmo coil, adding to the graduated look of these links as they get smaller going toward the back of the neckline.

13 Use your hands to create an S shape in the coiled area of wire (**Figure 8**). Then, with round-nose pliers, create an open spiral in toward the bends of the S (**Figure 9**). Stop short of completely turning the spiral into the center and flatten the edges with the chasing hammer again. You may need to pull the coil out a bit in order to do this—just be sure to turn the spiral into the center of the bends in the S after it's hammered. Make two. Set aside.

14 For the final links in the series, use 20-gauge brass to tightly coil around 1¼" (3.2 cm) of a 4" (10 cm) piece of 16-gauge brass. Trim excess 20-gauge wire. Use round-nose pliers to form a simple loop at one end of the 16-gauge wire and slide the coil up so that it meets the simple loop.

15 Form an arch in the coil of wire and then use round-nose pliers to form a spiral that bends in toward the coil (**Figure 10**). Again, stop short of meeting the coil with the spiral to flatten the wire with the chasing hammer and bench block. Then complete the spiral. Make two. Set aside.

16 The remaining eight jump rings will be used to connect the five coiled links. Lay out the links so that the coils alternate direction as they move from one side of the piece to the other. Connect each link to the next using two jump rings at each join. Set aside. (**Figure 11**)

17 Using a 3" (7.5 cm) piece of 16-gauge wire, make a hook clasp. Set aside.

18 Oxidize the brass (see page 27): Dampen a cotton ball with ammonia and seal all the components in the resealable bag with the paper towel. Seal the bag closed and allow the brass wire to darken. (about 1½ to 2 hours).

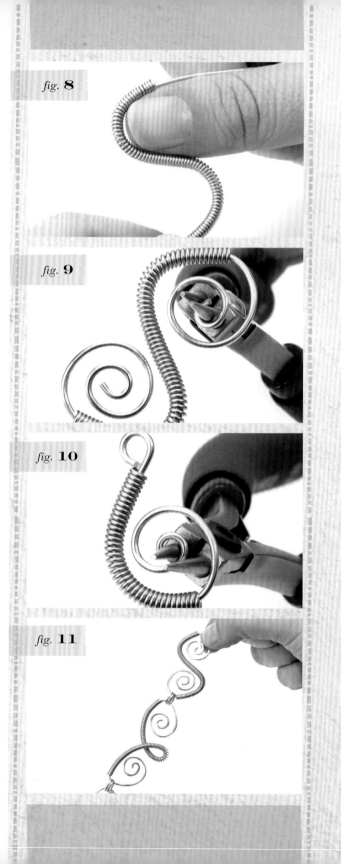

fig. **8**

fig. **9**

fig. **10**

fig. **11**

fig. **12**

COLOR MAKES IT YOUR OWN

This design can be created in any variety of colors for a completely different look and feel each time. Try it with sterling wire for the core and chain, with blue alcohol inks on the brass coils. Or how about copper with purple accents? Each piece will still be bold and grand, but the changes in color can be as unique as the woman wearing it.

19 With the polishing cloth, remove the tarnish from the darkened wire on all components to brighten the high points and leave shadows in the deep portions. Set aside.

20 Lay out the polished coiled piece of the necklace on the craft mat. Using the cranberry-colored alcohol ink, add patina to the coiled area of the links. Carefully turn the piece over to add the patina to the back side once the ink is dry.

21 Use the paintbrush and sealant to seal the patina. Once dry on the one side, remember to seal the opposite side as well. You only need to seal the areas of wire that have been tinted with the alcohol ink. Allow the sealant to dry and set.

22 Open the simple loop on the left end of the coiled component and attach it to the figure-eight links at one end of a length of the handmade chain from Step 3. Do the same to the opposite side as well. Then add the clasp to the length of chain that is short (the final jump ring).

23 Use chain-nose pliers to attach the dangles by opening their jump rings and closing them around the finished necklace. Attach the single dangles to each of the jump rings in the chains nearest the coiled components. Attach the double dangles to the second link in the coiled components. And finally, attach the pendant to the center loop. (**Figure 12**)

TECHNIQUES

Coiling

Wrapped loops

Simple loops

Patina

Ear wires

TOOLS

Round-nose pliers

Chain-nose pliers

Wire cutters

Ammonia

Salt water

Resealable container

MATERIALS

8" (20.5 cm) 20-gauge sterling silver wire

15" (38 cm) 20-gauge copper wire

3' (91.5 cm) 24-gauge copper wire

5" (12.7 cm) brass fine curb chain

Two 15mm lampwork-glass beads

*Lampwork beads by
Ali VandeGrift*

Finshed size: 3" (7.5 cm)

seahorse tales
EARRINGS

Amazingly small with such remarkable detail, the tiniest of sea creatures float effortlessly through the flowing currents. Seahorses listen keenly to mermaid whispers and spread rumors among curious crustaceans. Lend an ear to these inspired earrings and you may hear the story, too. The long length dusts your shoulder like a seahorse tapping for your attention.

fig. **1**

fig. **2**

1. Begin these earrings by making the coiled spirals that dangle at the very bottom of them. Cut two pieces of 20-gauge copper to 2" (5 cm). Tightly coil 1½" (3.8 cm) of the piece with 24-gauge copper wire. Trim excess wire.

2. Use round-nose pliers to spiral the coiled piece of wire. Form a simple loop with the remaining bare wire. Make two. (**Figure 1**)

3. Follow the method shown on page 28 to patina the spirals with ammonia and salt water. Once the patina has developed and has dried completely, seal with sealant. Set aside. (**Figure 2**)

4. Cut four pieces of chain 1¼" (3.2 cm) long. Set aside.

5. At one end of a 4" (10 cm) piece of 20-gauge wire, start to form a wrapped loop. Before closing the loop, attach it to two of the last links of the pieces of chain. Close the loop and then trim the excess wire.

6. Slide on a lampwork-glass bead and make another wrapped loop. Trim excess wire.

7. Holding the beaded link by the chain, dip the lampwork-beaded wire into liver of sulfur solution to lightly darken the wire. It won't take much for the wire to go from bright copper to a dull brown. Do not leave the bead in so long that the wire becomes black.

8. Open the simple loop of the coiled spiral with chain-nose pliers and attach it to the two free ends of chain. Close the loop.

9. Repeat Steps 5–7 for the second earring.

10. Attach your favorite style ear wire to the wrapped loop.

TECHNIQUES
Embroidery
Patina
Stamping

TOOLS
Round-nose pliers
Chain-nose pliers
Metal snips
Disc cutter
Dapping set
Punch pliers
Alphabet stamps
Bench block
Chasing hammer
Nylon mallet
Bracelet mandrel
¼" (6 mm) steel mandrel
Ammonia
Resealable container
Fine sandpaper
Round-nose needle file

MATERIALS
24-gauge sheet metal brass
4" (10 cm) 16-gauge brass wire
6" (15 cm) 18-gauge brass wire
18" (45.5 cm) 28-gauge sterling silver wire
One 30mm lampwork-glass cabochon
36" (91.4 cm) length of 3mm silk cord

Lampwork bead by Kerry Bogert

Finshed size: 7" (18 cm)

hidden grace
BRACELET

There is a New Year's tradition in which individuals choose a word to keep in mind throughout the coming year. The word is just for them, and it is usually something they want to seek out in their daily lives. Grace is a word I see come up quite often as the chosen word. Hidden on the back side of this cuff is stamped that word: Out of sight, but not out of mind.

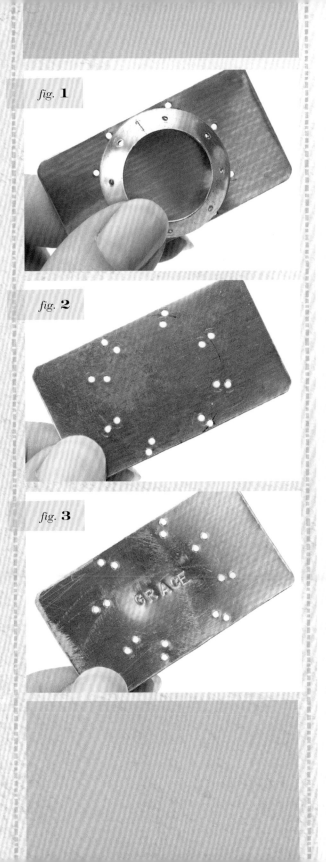

fig. **1**

fig. **2**

fig. **3**

1. Start this bracelet project by cutting out the three metal components that will be brought together in the final piece. Cut one rectangle 2⅛" (5.25 cm) x 1⅜" (3.5 cm) and two triangular shapes that are 1⅜" (3.5 cm) wide and taper to ½" (1.3 cm) along a 1½" (3.8 cm) distance, out of sheet metal brass using metal snips.

2. Round the edges of each metal piece and file any rough spots. Set aside.

3. Using the disc cutters, create a brass washer from the sheet metal that is 1¼" (3.2 cm) across with an inner area that is ¾" (2 cm) across.

4. Use the dapping set to bend the metal washer into a bezel shape that will fit over the lampwork cabochon.

5. With punch pliers, punch eight equally spaced holes around the edge of the shaped brass washer.

6. Center the shaped brass washer on the larger rectangular piece of brass. Use a pencil to outline the brass washer and mark the placement of the punched holes about ⅛" (2 mm) from those on the brass washer onto the rectangle of brass.

7. With the punch pliers, punch the eight holes marked on the brass rectangle (**Figure 1**). Also, punch eight matching holes just inside the pencil mark of the brass washer (**Figure 2**).

8. On the reverse side of the brass rectangle, stamp the word G R A C E (or another word with special meaning to you) on the metal with the alphabet stamps, bench block, and hammer. Center the word inside the inner ring of punch marks. (**Figure 3**)

9   Anchor an 18" (45.5 cm) piece of 28-gauge sterling silver wire to the back side of the brass rectangle and bring the wire up to the front of the work through one of the inner circle of punched holes and the coordinating hole in the washer. Bring the wire down through the outer hole on the brass plate, completing the stitch. Slip your lampwork cabochon between the washer and the rectangular plate. (**Figure 4**)

10 Continue stitching the brass washer to the brass rectangle, bringing the embroidery wire up through the coordinating punched holes and creating a bezel that holds the lampwork cabochon onto the brass rectangle. (**Figure 5**)

11 When you have reached the point where you started, pass the embroidery wire through the starting hole again, but do not come up through the hole in the brass washer. Instead, work the tail of wire out through a space between the washer and brass rectangle. Trim the excess wire and tuck the short tail back in between the washer and brass rectangle. Set aside.

12 Using the technique shown on page 20, make two jump rings on a ¼" (6 mm) steel mandrel using 18-gauge brass wire. Set aside.

13 With a 3" (7.5 cm) piece of 16-gauge wire, make an S-clasp. Add an extra detail by wrapping the center of the clasp with a piece of 28-gauge sterling silver wire.

14 Place all the brass bracelet components, including the jump rings and clasp, in ammonia fumes as shown in the patina technique (see page 27). Once brass has darkened, use a polishing cloth to highlight the jump rings and clasp.

fig. 4

fig. 5

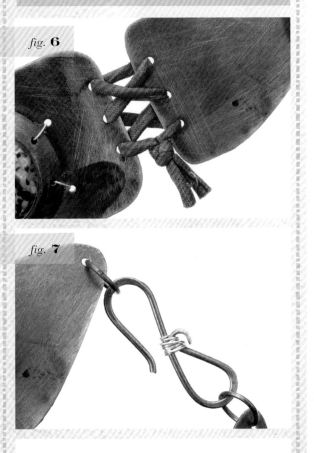

fig. **6**

fig. **7**

BEAUTIFUL BEZELS

I love the look of bezel-set beads, be they glass or gems. What I don't love is fighting with torches, flux, and solder to create hot-worked bezels. Wire embroidery is a wonderful solution for creating custom-sized cold-connection bezels. A set of disc cutters allows you to create the bezel walls in any size needed, the dapping set cups the wall to hold the bead, and your embroidery stitches that bezel wall to a backing. It really couldn't be simpler.

15 Use fine sandpaper to scuff up the surface and oxidation on the larger brass components. Focus your rubbing to the outer edges of the pieces and when working on the brass rectangle, be careful not to damage the glass cabochon.

16 With a pencil, lay out three equally spaced holes along the edges of the brass rectangle. Mark matching holes along the larger edge of each triangular brass piece. Use punch pliers to make a hole at each marking. Then use a round-nose needle file to open those holes to a slightly larger size. Also punch a single hole at the tapered end of each triangle piece.

17 Holding the brass rectangle against the bracelet mandrel, use a nylon mallet to gently hammer the edges of the rectangle to give the piece an arched shape. Do the same to the two triangular pieces of brass as well.

18 Take the silk cord and cut it in half (pieces should now be about 18″ [45.5 cm]). Thread one piece of silk through the holes on the edges of the brass rectangle and the brass triangle as you would to lace a corset or shoe. Tie a knot in the cording and trim excess. (**Figure 6**)

19 Repeat the lacing on the other side of the brass rectangle tying all the components together.

20 Using chain-nose pliers, open a jump ring. Close the jump ring after attaching it to the hole punched in the tapered end of one of the brass triangle pieces. Do this with the second jump ring and be sure to attach the clasp as well before closing the ring on the opposite side of the bracelet. (**Figure 7**)

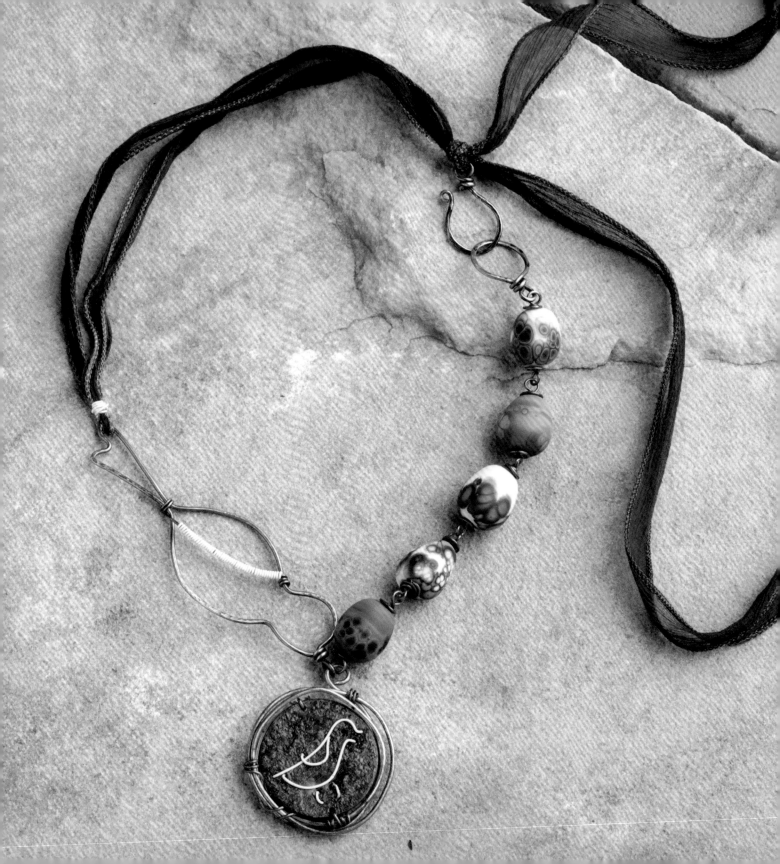

TECHNIQUES

Embroidery

Spiraling

Wrapped loops

Coiling

Clasps

Patina

TOOLS

Round-nose pliers

Chain-nose pliers

Wire cutters

Punch pliers

Chasing hammer

Bench block

½" (1.3 cm) mandrel

Ammonia

Cotton balls

Sealable plastic bag

Sealed container

Sawdust

Vinegar

Polishing cloth

Sealant

Paintbrush

MATERIALS

4' (1.2 m) 16-gauge brass wire

5' (1.5 m) 20-gauge brass wire

3' (91.5 cm) 24-gauge colored copper wire (color shown: ivory)

One 1¼" (3.2 cm) brass disc

Five 15mm lampwork-glass eggs

36" (95.1 cm) length of 4mm silk cord

Lampwork beads by Kelley Wenzel

Finished size: 19½" (49.5 cm)

tender nest
NECKLACE

"Tweet Tweet" chirps the little one, and mama bird is there to answer the call. In this nature-inspired piece, let your wire stitches embroider a sweet fledgling that captures a wonderful symbol of taking flight into the unknown and flourishing. A painted silk ribbon ties it all together bringing a supple softness to a tender nest.

Chick

1   To embroider the chick on the brass disc, sketch the outline of what will be embroidered, and lay out the holes to be pierced with punch pliers according to the diagram shown. Punch the holes. (**Figure 1**)

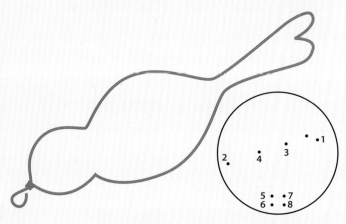

2   With a 12″ (30.5 cm) piece of 24-gauge ivory-colored copper wire, anchor the wire tail to the back of the work and bring the wire up through hole 1, and back down through hole 2. Mold the wire into an arch for the head and allow it to curve in to show the contour of the back. (**Figure 2**)

3   Bring the wire up through hole 1 and pass it back through hole 2. Shape this length into the belly of the chick.

4   Bring the wire to the front of the work through hole 3 and pass it into hole 4. This will become the chick's wing.

5   Bring the wire to the front of the work again through hole 5 and pass it into hole 6. Repeat with holes 7, then 8. These are the chick's legs. Punch one hole between the chick's legs that will later be used to secure the disc to the wire nest.

6   Once you have finished embroidering the chick, using the technique for creating a vinegar patina (shown on page 29), age the brass disc. Once the level of green patina you want is reached, remove the metal from the sawdust and vinegar and allow the disc to dry completely. (**Figure 3**)

fig. **1**

fig. **2**

fig. **3**

· RUSTIC *wrappings*

78

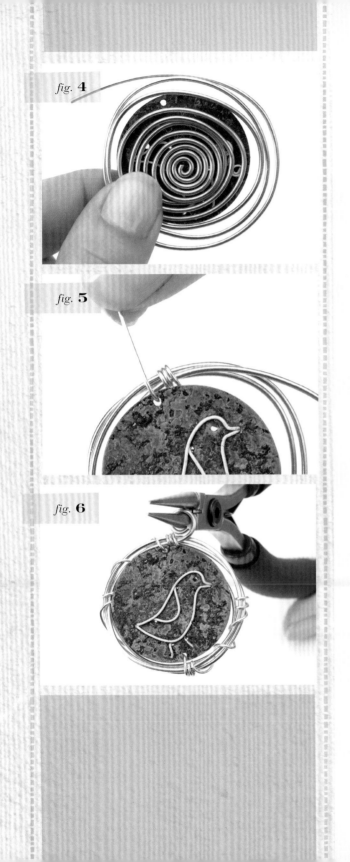

fig. 4

fig. 5

fig. 6

7　With metal sealant, seal the patina surface of the brass disc. It is important to allow the sealant to dry completely (overnight if possible). Set aside.

8　The embroidered chick needs a nest to settle in. With a 2′ (61 cm) piece of 16-gauge brass wire, create a large flat spiral with round-nose pliers. When the spiral becomes too large to be formed further with round-nose pliers, switch to chain-nose pliers. Allow the spiral to be loose and a bit random. Once the spiral is large enough to completely cover the back side of the embroidered disc, continue loosely spiraling the wire slightly larger than the outer edge of the disc. Finish with a simple loop. (**Figure 4**)

9　Use a 12″ (30.5 cm) piece of 20-gauge brass wire and secure the disc to the wire nest with a few wraps, and pass the wire through the top hole in the embroidered disc, and then wrap the nest a few more times. (**Figure 5**) Trim the excess wire and secure the embroidered disc in the same way through the bottom hole.

10　Add more wraps of 20-gauge brass wire near the simple loop of the nest and along the left edge as well. Trim excess wire. (**Figure 6**)

Mama Bird

11 To build the mother bird, use a 12″ (30.5 cm) piece of 16-gauge brass wire. Form a simple loop with round-nose pliers at one end and then, from there, use your round-nose pliers to shape the contours of the bird following the illustration provided. Wrap the end of the 16-gauge wire around the area just below the simple loop. Trim excess wire. (**Figure 7**)

12 With your chasing hammer and bench block, hammer flat the head, tail, and underbelly of the bird. Set aside.

13 Use 24-gauge ivory-colored copper wire to tightly coil 1½″ (3.8 cm) of a 6″ (15 cm) piece of 20-gauge brass wire. Trim excess ivory wire.

14 Wrap the 20-gauge coil-covered brass wire around the bird frame just behind the arch of the head (**Figure 8**). Wrap the other end of the brass wire around the tail, pulling the two tail wires together (**Figure 9**). Trim excess wire and form a gentle arch in the coil so the wire acts like the shape of a bird's wing. Set aside.

15 With 20-gauge brass wire, create a beaded chain of lampwork eggs using linked wrapped loops. When wrapping the loop closed, form a simple spiral with the wire that lies flat against the bead instead of just wrapping it twice. Set aside. (**Figure 10**)

Clasp

16 The two-part clasp consists of a large loop link and a matching exaggerated hook to catch it (**Figure 11**). To make the loop link, use a 3″ (7.5 cm) piece of 16-gauge wire. Start with a simple loop and then wrap the remaining wire around a ½″ (1.3 cm) mandrel and wrap closed like a wrapped loop.

17 For the clasp, start with a wrapped loop in a size similar to the simple loop of the loop link. Leave about 1¾″ (4.5 cm) wire remaining and wrap that around the ½″ (1.3 cm) mandrel. With round-nose pliers, turn a small loop at the end of the arch.

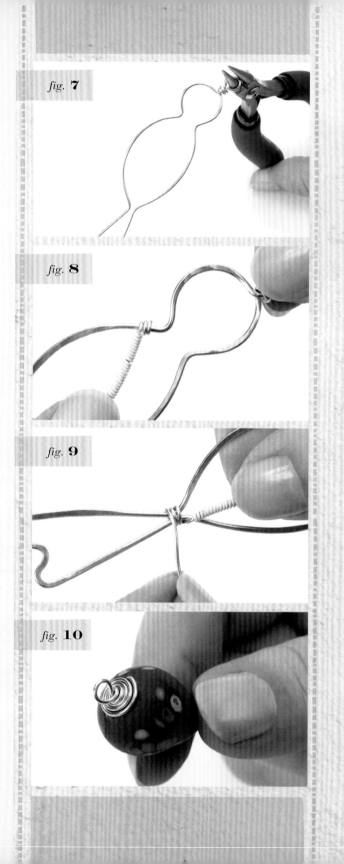

fig. **7**

fig. **8**

fig. **9**

fig. **10**

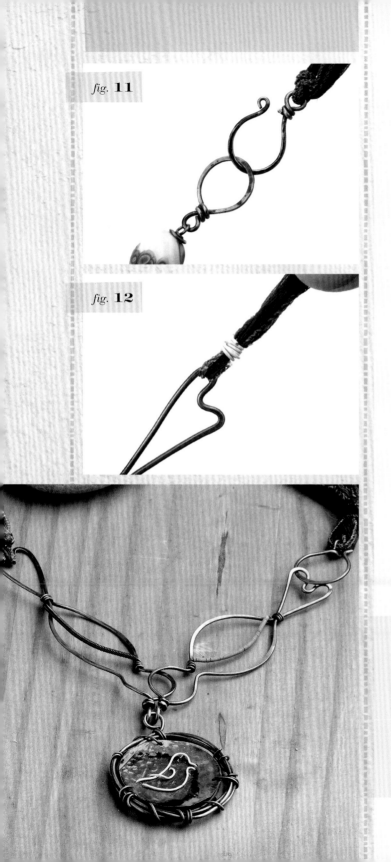

fig. **11**

fig. **12**

18 With your chasing hammer and bench block, flatten the loop and arch of the clasp. Set aside.

Patina and Assembly

19 Using the ammonia oxidation technique (see page 28), patina the wire bird, the embroidered wire nest, the beaded links, and the clasp. With the polishing cloth, buff back the patina to a soft aged look.

20 To assemble the necklace, use chain-nose pliers to open the simple loop on nest focal. Connect it to the last loop of the beaded links and to the simple loop of the wire bird. Close the loop.

21 Open the simple loop on the loop side of the clasp and connect it to the ending loop of the beaded links. Close the loop.

22 Run the silk cording through the tail feathers of the wire bird. With an 8" (20.5 cm) piece of ivory-colored copper wire, wrap the silk cord with wire. Trim the excess wire and use chain-nose pliers to tuck in the wire end. (**Figure 12**)

23 Bring the ends of the silk cord together and pass them through the wrapped loop on your clasp. Form a knot in the cording that locks the clasp onto the cording about 6" (15 cm) for the tail of the wire bird.

alternate view

Create this design featuring a mother and father bird tending the nest by making two of the wire bird links. Then, use brass figure-eight links to make a length of chain connecting to the clasp components. This nest was textured with a texture hammer, and then patina with alcohol inks was added.

TOOLS

Round-nose pliers

Wire cutters

Hole punch

Disc cutter

Dapping set

Chasing hammer

Bench block

Ring mandrel

Steel wool

Hydrogen peroxide

White vinegar

Salt

Ammonia

Cotton balls

Resealable bag

Shallow dish

Sealant

MATERIALS

4" (10 cm) 16-gauge annealed steel wire

24-gauge brass sheet metal

6" (15 cm) 20-gauge brass wire

Two 10mm small hollow lamp-work-glass beads

Lampwork beads by Kerry Bogert

Finshed size: 2" (5 cm)

luna unearthed
EARRINGS

Created in tribute to a dear friend, these ancient-seeming earrings are created with golden glowing glass orbs. Moonlight is swept up in bends of her hair and dances as it reflects off the glossy surface of the beads. The metal has been rusted to appear acquainted with the passage of many a moon.

fig. 1

fig. 2

1. Begin this earring design by creating the small brass bead caps that cover the holes on either side of the lampwork beads. To do so, use the disc cutter to make four ¼" (6 mm) discs.

2. With the punch pliers, make a hole in the center of each of the four discs and then use the dapping set to cup the discs into the cap shape. Set aside. (**Figure 1**)

3. Flush cut the ends of two 2" (5 cm) pieces of 16-gauge steel. Use the steel wool to remove the carbon coating on the surface of the steel wire.

4. With the chasing hammer and bench block, flatten ⅛" (3 mm) of one end of the steel wire. Slide one bead cap, one lampwork hollow bead, and another bead cap onto the steel wire. (**Figure 2**)

5. Using round-nose pliers, form a simple loop at one end of steel wire where it has been flattened. Set aside.

6. Repeat Steps 4 and 5 for the second earring.

7. Using the patina recipe for rusting steel (see page 32), mix the hydrogen peroxide, white vinegar, and salt in a shallow bowl. Soak both earring components in the patina solution and allow time for patina to form.

8. While the earring dangle components are developing patina, make the ear wire from which they will dangle. Form a wrapped loop at the end of a 3" (7.5 cm) piece of 20-gauge brass wire.

9. Wrap the ear wire around a ring mandrel to form a large loop. Use chain-nose pliers to bend the wrapped loop down from the ring of the larger loop. Trim the tail of the wire so that there is about ¼" (6 mm) of space between the wire end and the wrapped loop.

10 Use the chasing hammer and bench block to flatten the large loop of the ear wire. Set aside.

11 Repeat Steps 8–10 for the second ear wire.

12 Place ear wires in a resealable bag containing cotton balls soaked in ammonia. Seal the bag and allow the brass to darken. Once oxidized, remove the brass from the bag and lightly polish. Set aside.

13 Once the rust patina has formed on the steel components, remove them from the patina solution and allow to dry.

14 When all the pieces of the components are dry, lightly seal the steel with a layer of sealant.

15 Very carefully open the simple loop of the dangle component, just enough to slip it onto the wrapped loop of an ear wire and close the loop. Repeat for the second earring. (**Figure 3**)

fig. **3**

A NOTE ON COLOR

This is one of those projects that would look lovely in any color. By simply changing the color of the transparent glass used in the lampwork beads, you can change the overall feel of the earrings. When changing the color, you should think about changing the metal as well. If the beads are warm shades of red, orange, or yellow, this rusty steel and brass look fits perfect. However, when using cool shades of green, blue, or purple, try mixing it with unrusted steel and sterling accents.

Embroidery

Wrapped loops

Clasps

Patina

TOOLS

Chain-nose pliers

Round-nose pliers

Wire cutters

Punch pliers

Alphabet stamps

Utility hammer

Liver of sulfur

Polishing cloth

MATERIALS

10' (3.1 m) 20-gauge sterling silver wire

½" (1.3 mm) wide 20-gauge sterling silver strip

4" (10 cm) length of 24-gauge colored copper wire (color shown: turquoise)

Four 8mm lampwork-glass round beads

Lampwork beads by Kerry Bogert

Finshed size: 7½" (19 cm)

wonder while you wander BRACELET

While out on an unexpected afternoon stroll, your feet move one in front of the other, and your thoughts are open to wander and drift to far-off places. It is too easy to forget to let thoughts wander when life is so full of stresses, though. Let this embroidered cuff be a reminder to just let go and see where your mind goes.

1 Prepping the strip of sterling silver that will be featured at the center of this cuff is the starting point for this design. Using alphabet stamps, hammer the letters W O N D E R W H I L E Y O U W A N D E R into the metal. I recommend starting with the center letters, L and E. Then work out in either direction. Don't worry about keeping the letters on the same plane. Allowing some letters to float higher or lower adds to the detail of this piece.

2 Once finished stamping the words, mark the holes needed to add the embroidered edge to the metal strip. Place each mark ¼" (6 mm) apart across the top and bottom. Use punch pliers to pierce the holes in the metal. (**Figure 1**)

3 Using a long piece of colored copper wire, anchor one end of wire to the back of the metal strip and begin embroidering a blanket-stitch edge to the piece. (**Figure 2**) You will go into each hole three times before trailing the wire over to the next hole. (**Figure 3**) If at any point your wire breaks, anchor the tail on the back side and start with a new piece.

TIP: I didn't specify a specific length of wire for this step because you should start with a length that you are comfortable with. I was able to work this edge with one piece of 10' (305 cm) long wire, but it took a great deal of patience, and I had to make sure the wire didn't kink on me. I suggest starting with a 2' (61 cm) length, then if you think you can handle more, try longer lengths.

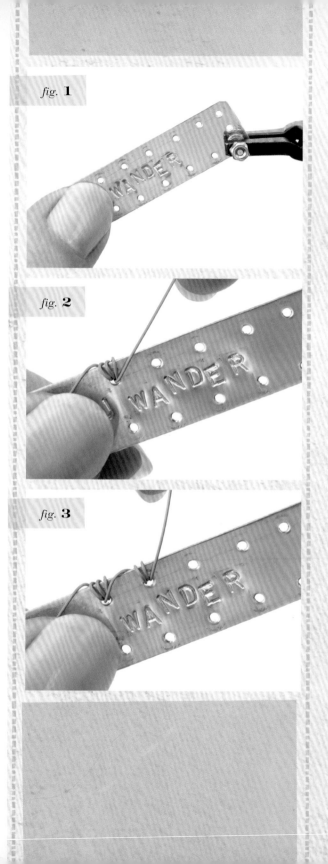

fig. **1**

fig. **2**

fig. **3**

fig. **4**

4   Once the embroidered edge on this design is complete, the rest of it comes together quickly. Use punch pliers to add a single hole at each end of the metal strip.

5   With round-nose pliers and using 20-gauge sterling silver wire, create beaded links with chunky wrapped loops. You will connect two beaded links together for each side of the cuff, and one of the chunky wrapped loops should attach to the holes punched in Step 4. (**Figure 4**)

6   In place of a wrapped loop, form the hook of your clasp with wire at the end of one of the bead link duos.

7   Soak the cuff in liver of sulfur to oxidize (see page 26) and then polish back the oxidation with a polishing cloth.

alternative view

For this variation, I focused on mixing two types of the same metal, copper and colored copper. Make simple figure-eight chain from copper in place of beads. The embroidered edge of the copper word strip has been done with ivory-colored copper wire.

TECHNIQUES

Wrapped loops

Coiling

Jump rings

Clasps

Patina

TOOLS

Round-nose pliers

Chain-nose pliers

Wire cutters

¼" (6 mm) mandrel

Ammonia

Cotton balls

Resealable bag

Polishing cloth

MATERIALS

6' (1.8 m) 18-gauge brass wire

8" (20.5 cm) 20-gauge brass wire

12" (30.5 cm) 24-gauge anodized color copper wire (color shown: purple)

Lock plate

Sari-silk cording

Four 15mm barrel-shaped boro lampwork beads

Lampwork beads by Melissa Rediger

Finshed size: 8½" (21.5 cm)

safe passage
BRACELET

In our not too distant past, many trips across the sea were taken by boat rather than plane. I love to imagine grand trunks filled with passengers' belongings being wheeled into luxurious staterooms. I found this little brass lock plate at a local salvage shop, and I can't help but wonder if it might have been on one of those travel trunks at one time or another.

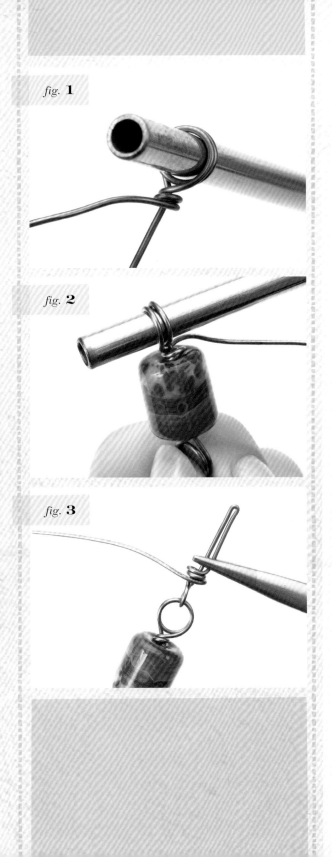

fig. **1**

fig. **2**

fig. **3**

1   Coil the 18-gauge brass wire around the ¼" (6 mm) mandrel at least ten times. Following the jump ring technique on page 20, trim to coil into eight jump rings. Set aside.

2   To create the beaded links, use an 8" (20.5 cm) piece of 18-gauge brass wire. Wrap the wire around the ¼" (6 mm) mandrel twice, one length of wire around the other, as you would to close a wrapped loop. Trim the excess wrapped wire and slide the piece off the mandrel. (**Figure 1**)

3   Add a lampwork barrel bead to the wire link. With chain-nose pliers, form a 45-degree bend in the wire and again wrap it around the ¼" (6 mm) mandrel. Wrap the tail of wire around the lead wire near the bead as you did before. Trim the excess wire and set aside. (**Figure 2**)

4   Repeat Steps 2 and 3 with the remaining three lampwork beads for a total of four links. Set aside.

5   To make the clasp, use a 6" (15 cm) piece of 18-gauge wire. Form a wrapped loop at one end of the wire and before closing the loop, attach it to one of the beaded links. Trim the excess wrapped wire.

6   About 1" (2.5 cm) from the wrapped area of the clasp, form a hairpin bend in the wire bringing two wires side by side. Grip the parallel wires with chain-nose pliers and with your free hand, wrap the tail of wire over top of the first wrapping. Trim the excess wire. (**Figure 3**)

7   With round-nose pliers, form the two parallel wires into a hook. Set aside.

8 The small wire key will be made from an 8" (20.5 cm) piece of 20-gauge brass wire. Start by using round-nose pliers to make the three scrolls about 2" (5 cm) from one end of the wire. Bring the scrolls together to create a small floret shape and wrap the short end of wire around the long end as you would a wrapped loop (**Figure 4**). Trim the excess wrapped wire.

9 Hammer flat the arches of the floret with the chasing hammer and bench block.

10 On the opposite end, using chain-nose pliers, form a series of bends that resemble the teeth on the end of a skeleton key. Wrap the tail of the wire back around the key shaft just past the color wire coil. Trim the excess wire. Hammer flat the teeth of the key with the chasing hammer and bench block. (**Figure 5**)

11 Tightly coil ½" (1.3 cm) of what will be the shaft of the key with colored copper wire.

12 Create an oxidized patina for the brass (see page 27): Seal the key, beaded links, and jump rings in a resealable bag with a cotton ball soaked in ammonia. Allow the brass to darken and then remove from the bag.

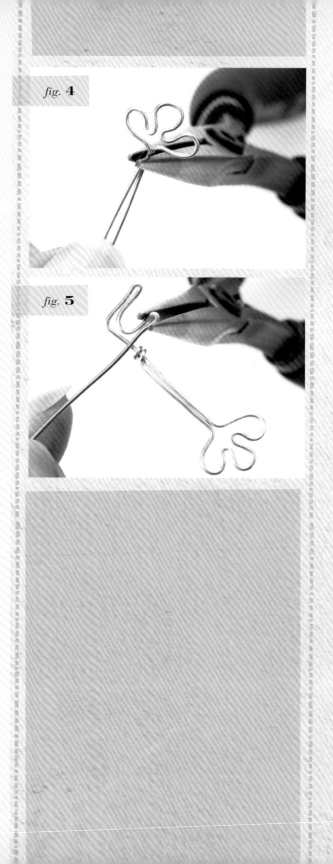

fig. **4**

fig. **5**

fig. **6**

13 Using chain-nose pliers, open a jump ring and attach two beaded links together. Close the jump ring. Repeat with a second jump ring. (This looks like the link is doubled to match the beaded links.)

14 Continue connecting the beaded links with two jump rings at each junction until all the links have been attached. You should have your wire clasp at one end and the loop of a beaded link at the other.

15 Open another jump ring and attach it to the last beaded link. Before closing it, connect to one of the holes in the key plate and the floret of the wire key. Close the jump ring and do the same with a second jump ring. (**Figure 6**)

16 Use a polishing cloth to remove the tarnish from the brass.

17 Finish by knotting a piece of sari-silk cording to the key plate through the hole that connects the plate to the beaded links.

alternate view

This link style also looks lovely working as a chain link, *sans* the beads. To get this look, simply leave out the bead and when wrapping the second double loop, wrap the wire over the top of the first wrapping in a chunky style. Attach links to each other with jump rings as shown previously and finish with another snippet of sari-silk cording.

TECHNIQUES

Coiling

Head pins

Patina

TOOLS

Chasing hammer

Wire cutters

Bench block

Punch pliers

Bracelet mandrel

Liver of sulfur

Polishing cloth

Rotary tumbler

MATERIALS

8.5" (21.5 cm) 16-gauge sterling silver wire (per bangle)

2' (61 cm) 20g colored (for small trapped coil) or 10' 20g colored (5' of each of two colors for two-tone)

10' (3 m) 20-gauge sterling silver wire

3½" hole lampwork-glass rings

5 lampwork-glass head pins

Lampwork bead by Kerry Bogert

*Finished size: 8" (20.5 cm)
(These are made large enough to slip over your hand.)*

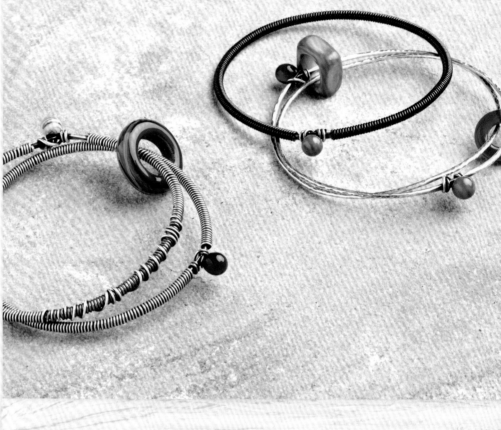

lilacs & peonies
BANGLES

Imagine an early summer day, just before it rains, when the air is heavy with the fragrant scents of lilacs and peonies. The gathering storm clouds cast shadows that make the colorful blooms appear to glow. Now, catch the essence of that day in a romantic collection of bangles. Each design builds on the next, adding depth and dimension to the finished set.

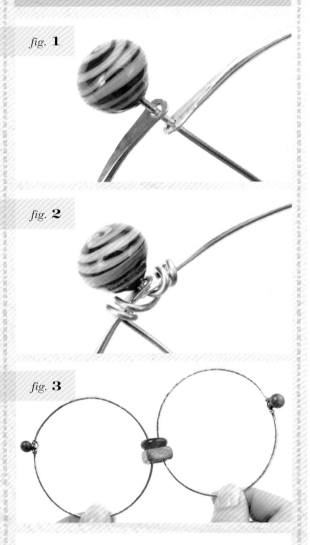

fig. **1**

fig. **2**

fig. **3**

COULD YOU USE A COILING GIZMO FOR THIS PROJECT?

Yes, if you were making this for a smaller wrist. Simply make the coil first, before hammering the ends and adding the holes. However, for the size shown, a Coiling Gizmo would not work because the coils are only about 7" (18 cm) at their longest. These call for 8" (20.5 cm) of coiling. Besides, I really like the look of a tightly wrapped coil for this project. The Coiling Gizmo would not hug the wire as nicely.

Simple Bangle

1   With the chasing end of your hammer, flatten ¼" (6 mm) of both ends of an 8½" (21.5 cm) piece of 16-gauge sterling wire. Once flattened, file smooth the ends and use punch pliers to put a hole in each flattened area. Make two.

2   Wrap the 16-gauge wire around a bracelet mandrel or other round object to form a circle. Be sure that the ends of the wire overlap each other.

3   Add two lampwork-glass rings to the coiled wire. (These will later connect the two bangles together.)

4   Slip a lampwork-glass head pin through the holes in the ends of the wire locking the bangle in its circular shape. The head of the head pin should be sitting on the outside of the circle (**Figure 1**). Wrap the wire tail of the head pin around the 16-gauge wire twice on one side of the glass head and then again on the other side (**Figure 2**).

5   Trim excess wire and file smooth.

6   Repeat Steps 2–5 for the second wire, slipping the wire through the same two lampwork-glass rings used in Step 3. (**Figure 3**)

7   With the ball-peen end of the chasing hammer, texture the entire circumference of the bangle against the bench block. Be sure to keep your glass beads held away from where your hammer is striking. Repeat for the second bangle. Set aside.

Coiled Bangle

1 Prep the bangle as you did in Step 1 of the Simple Bangle.

2 With an 8½′ (274 cm) piece of 20-gauge sterling wire, tightly coil the 16-gauge wire working from one end to the other. Leave about ⅜″ (1 cm) of each end exposed. Trim excess wire and file smooth.

3 Repeat Steps 2–5 of the Simple Bangle with the coil-covered piece of 16-gauge wire. After the circle is formed, but before you secure it with a head pin, slip one lampwork-glass ring onto the wire. Set aside. (**Figure 4**)

Trapped Coil Bangle

1 Again, prep the bangle as you did in Step 1 of the Simple Bangle.

2 Using a 2′ (61 cm) piece of 20-gauge colored copper wire, tightly coil a 2″ (5 cm) area near the center of the 16-gauge wire. Trim excess wire and file smooth.

3 Using a 6′ (183 cm) piece of 20-gauge sterling wire, tightly coil around the 16-gauge wire beginning at one end. When you reach the colored coil, loosely wrap the silver wire over the top of the colored wire (**Figure 5**). Then continue tightly coiling the 16-gauge wire with the remaining 20-gauge silver. Trim excess and file smooth.

4 Repeat Steps 2–5 of the Simple Bangle with the coil-covered piece of 16-gauge wire. After the circle is formed, but before you secure it with a head pin, slip one end through the lampwork-glass ring of the Coiled Bangle. This will connect the two bangles together (**Figure 6**). Set aside.

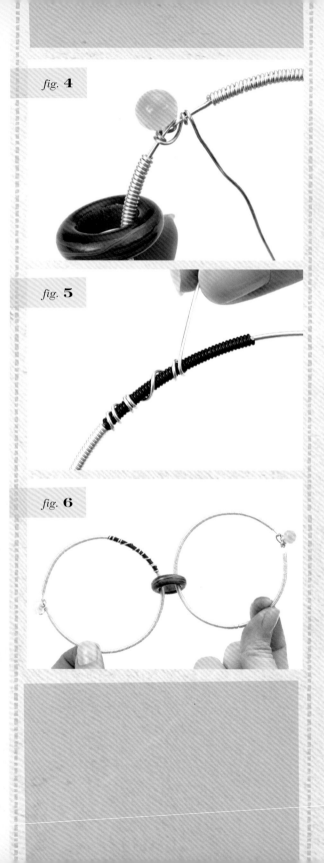

fig. **4**

fig. **5**

fig. **6**

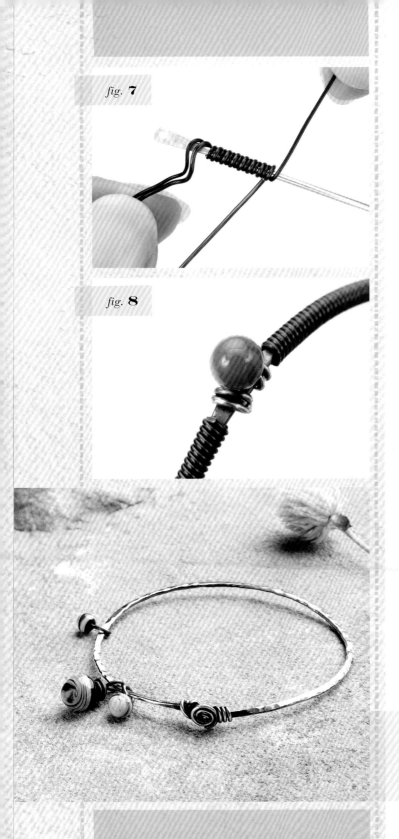

fig. **7**

fig. **8**

Two-Tone Coil Bangle

1   As with the previous bangles created for this project, begin by prepping the bangle as you did in Step 1 of the Simple Bangle.

2   Secure two 4.5′ (137 cm) lengths of 20-gauge colored wires (both purple and magenta) at one end of the 16-gauge wire. Alternate back and forth between each color of wire to tightly coil the length of the 16-gauge wire (**Figure 7**). Trim excess and file smooth.

TIP: This step can be a bit tedious, but it is so worth the effort. Work with plenty of elbow room, keep a firm grip on your wire as you go, and before you know it, you'll have that whole core wire beautifully wrapped.

3   Repeat Steps 2, 4, and 5 of the Simple Bangle (**Figure 8**). Set aside.

Create the Finish

1   Oxidize all five bangles in liver of sulfur (see page 26).

2   With a polishing cloth, buff the blackened area of sterling wire. You will see the colored copper wire kept its color.

3   Tumble bangles in a rotary tumbler for 30 minutes.

alternate view

Substitute wire swirl head pins for lampwork-glass head pins.

TECHNIQUES

Wrapped loops

Jump rings

Clasps

Embroidery

TOOLS

Round-nose pliers

Chain-nose pliers

Wire cutters

Scissors

Chasing hammer

Bench block

Resin

Sponge or disposable paintbrush

Plastic bag

Ammonia

Paper towel

Resealable bag

Punch pliers

Pencil

MATERIALS

11.25' (3.4 m) 18-gauge brass wire

2.5' (76 cm) 24-gauge colored copper wire (color shown: teal)

Two 1.25" (3.8 cm) brass discs

Two 1" (2.5 cm) brass discs

16" (40.6 cm) length of brass chain

One 18mm lampwork-glass daisy bead

Old book pages

Lampwork beads by Kerry Bogert

Finshed size: 18" (45.5 cm)

lazy daisy
NECKLACE

He loves me, he loves me not. How many afternoons as a young girl did you spend plucking daisy petals? The lazy daisy stitch is an embroidery classic that has a history dating back hundreds of years. Makes one wonder just how many hearts have been lost to the predictions of those tiny little petals.

*I find the best papers to resin are those
found in older books. Modern papers
tend to be more heavily bleached and
chemically treated; they just don't look
as nice when coated in resin as vintage
ones. Be on the lookout for old tattered
books at garage sales. I find most of
mine for less than a dollar. The old and
more yellowed the better! Vintage papers take on a lovely transparent quality when the resin is set that is wonderful when added to rustic designs.*

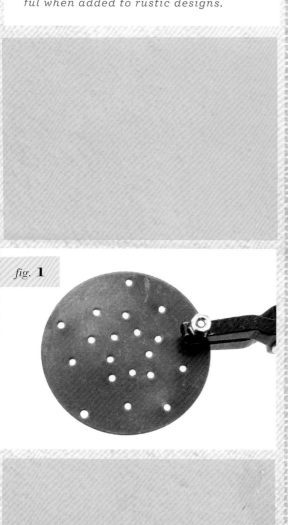

fig. **1**

Make Petals

1   We'll begin this design by creating the resin-coated
paper petals that dangle along this necklace. Cut
twenty-five pieces of 18-gauge brass wire each 5″
(12.5 cm) long.

2   With round-nose pliers, create a petal-shaped
wrapped loop at one end of the wire, leaving a
straight tail of wire about 2.5″ (6.5 cm) long. Trim
the excess wrapped wire, but not the tail wire. Repeat for all twenty-five pieces of wire.

TIP: There is no need to worry about making every petal
the exact same size and shape. Real petals are unique and
your handmade ones should be as well.

3   With the chasing hammer and bench block, hammer
the wire petal loop flat. Repeat for all twenty-five
petal loops.

4   Mix resin following the manufacturer's instructions.
Use the plastic bag as your work surface. Randomly
rip small pieces of paper slightly larger than the
wire petals. Use the sponge to coat each side of the
paper with resin.

5   After the paper is coated in resin, dip the wire petal
in the resin, and then lay the resin paper against
the flattened edge of the wire petal. Set aside on a
box or other object that allows the resin petal to be
suspended so that the resin can cure. Repeat for all
twenty-five petals.

TIP: The amount of time it takes for the resin to cure can
vary depending on the type of resin you are using. Some
dry within a few hours, and others need overnight. I use Ice
Resin and usually allow the resin to cure overnight.

Create the Daisy Pendant

6   While allowing the resin to cure on the paper petals,
create the daisy pendant. Use a pencil to lay out
the holes that need to be punched in both the large
and small brass discs. You will use just one of each
size. The larger disc will feature a full daisy, and the
smaller disc shows just half of one (see illustration
for hole layout). Use punch pliers to create holes
after they have been marked on the brass. (**Figure 1**)

7 Anchor an 18″ (45.5 cm) piece of 24-gauge colored copper wire to the back side of your larger daisy disc, holding it securely between the thumb and index finger of your nondominant hand. Come through hole 1 to the front of your work, form a small loop of wire by going back through hole 1, then come back up through hole 2, wrap around the top of that first loop, and go back into hole 2, tacking down the first petal. (See illustration for hole numbers.) (**Figure 2**)

8 Continue creating the inner circle of petals. If at any point your wire breaks, simply back up to the last point it was on the wrong side of your work, anchor it under one of the wires, and start with a new piece. (**Figure 3**)

TIP: As your wire travels in and out of the holes in your metal, some of the colored coating may be stripped from the wire. Personally, I like this look. I think it adds another layer to the work, giving the design highlights and shadows. If you want to avoid stripping the wire, use a file to clean any sharp edges caused by the punch pliers.

9 The outer layer of petals is created using the same method as the inner round. These holes have been labeled using letters in place of numbers to avoid petal confusion. Once all petals have been made, anchor the tail of your wire to the wrong side of your work. Trim excess. Set aside. (**Figure 4**)

10 Repeat the technique in Steps 2–4 with the second, smaller disc. There are three inner petals and two outer petals for this daisy. Set aside.

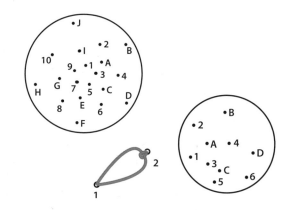

fig. **2**

fig. **3**

fig. **4**

WHY DO YOU NEED TO ADD BLANK DISCS TO THE BACK SIDE OF YOUR EMBROIDERY?

The wirework on the reverse side of the disc is really not flattering, and you wouldn't want it rubbing against your skin. Adding the plain disc hides the wild wire and gives your piece a professional finish. You could take things a step further and use alphabet stamps to write a message in the metal as well.

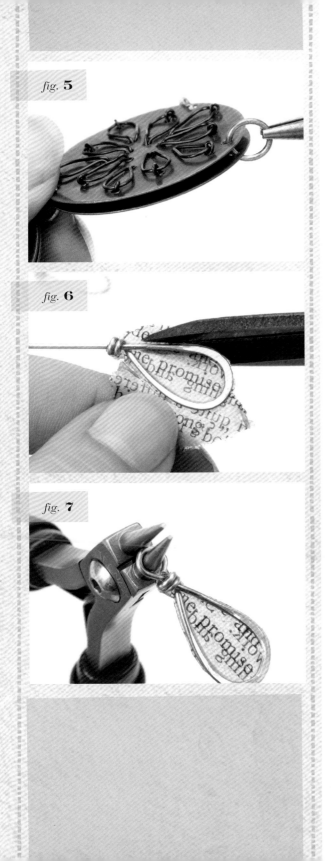

fig. 5

fig. 6

fig. 7

Assembly

11 With a 3" (7.5 cm) piece of 18-gauge brass wire, make a small coil of wire using the round-nose pliers. From the coil, cut three jump rings using a wire cutter. Set aside. *Note:* This is one of the few times that a mandrel isn't necessary to make a coil. Since you only need three jump rings, making a coil with pliers is a much faster way to go.

12 Look at your large embroidered daisy disc and decide which way you want it oriented. On either side of the top part of the larger pendant, punch two holes about ¾" (2 cm) apart. Punch one hole in the bottom center. Place the embroidered disc on top of the same-size plain one. Use a pencil to transfer markings for the holes just created and punch the plain disc in those spots.

13 Just two holes are needed in the small embroidered disc: one at the top, one at the bottom. Use your punch pliers to add those holes and then mark a same-size plain disc with pencil before punching the matching holes.

14 Use two chain-nose pliers to open the brass jump rings from Step 6. Hold the plain metal disc against the back side of your embroidered disc, line up the holes, and add a jump ring to the right and left sides of the pendant. Close the jump rings once they are attached. (**Figure 5**)

15 When adding the jump ring to the bottom hole in your large disc, you need to attach the lower half of the pendant as well. Attach the jump ring to the holes in the larger disc first, then, before closing the jump ring, add the small plain disc and the small embroidered disc.

16 Add 8" (20.5 cm) of brass chain to each side of the pendant by opening the last link in the chain as you would a jump ring. Set aside.

Finish the Petals

17 Once the resin petals have completely cured, use the scissors to trim the excess paper that is around the outside of the wire petal (**Figure 6**). Use wire cutters to trim the tail wire on a resin petal to ½" (1.3 cm). With the round-nose pliers, form a simple loop (**Figure 7**).

18   Repeat Step 17 for all twenty-five resin petals.

19   Make one flat spiral head pin from four 4" (10 cm) pieces of 18-gauge bronze-colored copper wire. Add a lampwork-glass flower bead to the head pin and make a large wrapped loop from the remaining length of wire. This will be used as the hook for the clasp of your finished piece. (**Figure 8**)

20   With a piece of 18-gauge brass, make a simple hook clasp with brass wire using round-nose pliers.

21   Soak a cotton ball in ammonia and place it in the resealable bag, along with the resin petals and wire clasp components. Allow the brass to darken, then remove from the bag and polish lightly.

22   With the chain-nose pliers, open the simple loop and attach the resin petal to a link in the chain next to the pendant. Attach twelve to the left side and twelve to the right side of the chain. (**Figure 9**)

23   Attach the last remaining resin petal to the holes previously punched in the bottom of the small pendant.

24   To complete the design by the wire clasp made from 18-gauge brass wire, use chain-nose pliers to open the last link of the chain on one side of the necklace and attach the lampwork beaded part of the clasp. Attach the hook part of the clasp to the opposite side of the necklace.

fig. **8**

fig. **9**

spice traders
EARRINGS

Watching passersby strolling through the aisles of an open-air market, where baskets of bold spices fill the air and tantalize the senses, the shrewd traders wait— demanding the best prices for their special fare, only willing to exchange goods if the return is right. These bohemian-inspired earrings call to the dealer, but the wearer is never willing to swap.

TECHNIQUES

Patina

Embroidery

Jump rings

Ear wires

TOOLS

Round-nose pliers

Chain-nose pliers

Wire cutters

Punch pliers

Disc cutters

Chain hammer

Bench block

Craft mat

Gesso

Paintbrush

Alcohol ink (colors shown are stream, meadow, lettuce, latte)

Sealant

Liver of sulfur

Polishing cloths

MATERIALS

18" (45.5 cm) 18-gauge sterling silver wire

6" (15 cm) 20-gauge sterling silver wire

3' (91.5 cm) 26-gauge colored copper wire

24-gauge brass sheet metal

Two 42mm ornate brass discs

1 g size 11° glass seed beads

Finshed size: 2½" (6.5 cm)

103

1. Create an alcohol ink patina on your brass discs (see page 31). Placing the ornate brass discs on your craft mat, begin these earrings by painting a thin layer of gesso on the surface of the metal discs. Allow the paint to dry completely.

2. Randomly dip alcohol inks onto the gesso surface of the metal discs, dipping one drop at a time and allowing the ink to spread across the surface. Allow the inks to dry completely.

3. Once the color patina has dried, paint a layer of sealant over the inked surface and allow this to dry completely.

4. While waiting for the sealant to cure on the metal discs, using the technique shown on page 20, make ten jump rings from 18-gauge sterling silver wire.

5. Once all the rings have been cut, place them and two 3" (7.5 cm) pieces of 20-gauge sterling silver in liver of sulfur to oxidize. Remove from the solution and lightly polish. Set aside.

6. Next, cut six ¼" (6 mm) discs from the brass sheet metal. Set aside.

7. When the sealant on the inked discs is completely dry, you are ready to start embroidering the design. With punch pliers, punch a series of eight holes at symmetrical points around the edges of the metal's center design. The embroidery will echo that design. Also punch five holes along the bottom edge of the metal. (**Figure 1**)

8. Anchor the end of an 18" (45.5 cm) piece of 26-gauge colored copper wire to the back of the metal disc. Bring the wire up through to the front of the work. Feed the wire end back through to the back of the work via the next hole in the series. Use your thumb to put a gentle arc in the wire.

9. Bring the wire back through to the front of the wire via the third hole in the series and then bring it back through to the back of the work via the second hole. Again, form a gentle arc in the wire with your thumb (**Figure 2**). Bring the wire to the front of the work through the third hole again and this time, to the back of the work through the fourth hole.

fig. **1**

fig. **2**

fig. **3**

fig. **4**

10   Continue working around the center of the metal disc until your embroidery reaches the starting point. Anchor the tail of the wire to the back of the work. Use chain-nose pliers to pinch the points where the wire threads in and out. (**Figure 3**)

11   Repeat Steps 7–10 and 9 for the second earring.

12   Attach the jump rings to the holes punched along the bottom edge of the inked metal discs. Center three jump rings with brass discs and the rings with a single glass seed bead on the outer edges. (**Figure 4**)

13   Use the chasing hammer and bench block to flatten ⅛" (3 mm) of the end of the oxidized pieces of 20-gauge sterling silver wire.

14   With round-nose pliers, form a small loop with the hammered end of the wire and before closing the loop, slide the inked disc component onto the wire. Close the loop. Form the remaining length of wire into a hook. Repeat for the second earring.

15   Trim excess wire on the ear hook and use the chasing hammer and bench block to hammer the arch of the ear wire. Repeat for the second earring.

BLENDING INKS

One of the things I love about working with alcohol inks is the way the ink will randomly spread across the surface of metal. Just a few drops can cover a large surface and naturally blend into one another. When you are adding your drops of ink to the surface of any project, keep in mind those kindergarten color lessons because the same applies to these inks. Blue and yellow will blend into green, yellow and red into orange, and red and blue will become purple. I find it is these blurred and blended areas of colors that have the most beautiful tones and make for truly unique finished pieces.

TECHNIQUES

Coiling

Jump rings

Clasps

Patina

TOOLS

Round-nose pliers

Chain-nose pliers

Wire cutters

Crimping pliers

⅜" (9 mm) mandrel

Liver of sulfur

Extrafine steel wool

Rotary tumbler

MATERIALS

8.5' (2.6 m) 16-gauge copper wire

12' (3.6 m) 20-gauge colored copper wire in four colors (colors shown: ivory, purple, orange, lavender)

14' (4.2 m) 22-gauge colored copper wire (color shown: vintage brass)

16' (4.8 m) 22-gauge sterling silver wire

Steel beading wire

Two crimp beads

Two wire guards

Twelve 18–20mm lampwork-glass hollow beads

Two 15mm lampwork-glass cone beads

Two 8mm round copper beads

Lampwork beads by Kerry Bogert

Finished size: 18" (45.5 cm)

swiftly bound NECKLACE

The brisk winds of fall bring with them a need for extra layers and thick wool sweaters. Gone are the days of tank tops and cute pendants. It is time for a piece of jewelry as substantial as it is beautiful. Large torch-worked hollow beads are accented by coiled-wire love knots creating a design that mimics balls of yarn . . . maybe the same yarn used to knit your favorite wool sweater.

1 Start this project by creating all the wire love knots that float between each hollow bead. Cut six 14" (35.5 cm) lengths of 16-gauge copper wire. Coil ivory-colored wire over about 12" (30.5 m) of one of the 16-gauge pieces of wire. Repeat with the other colored wires and sterling wire, making six coiled pieces of 16-gauge wire in a total of six different colors. Trim excess colored wire and set aside.

2 Coil one of the 16-gauge coil-covered pieces of wire around the ⅜" (1 cm) mandrel. Remove the coil from the mandrel and cut into rings (as if making jump rings on a larger scale). (**Figure 1**) You should get five to seven rings per piece. Repeat this with the other coil-covered wires for a total of thirty-nine rings.

3 With chain-nose pliers, open one ring and link it to another one. Be sure to close both rings well so that they look like continuous coils. Holding the two connected rings so they are side by side, add a third ring to the set by going through the center of the first two rings. (**Figure 2**)

4 Repeat Step 3 with the other coiled rings until you have a total of thirteen ring knots. Mix things up and use different combinations of colors to make each set of three a little different. Set aside.

5 Pass a ¹⁄₁₆" (2 mm) piece of steel beading wire through a crimp bead, a wire guard, and back through the crimp bead. Crimp. String one copper bead, one lampwork-cone bead, a ring knot, and a lampwork hollow bead. (**Figure 3**)

6 Continue alternating the ring knots and lampwork hollows. Then finish with a ring knot, one lampwork-cone bead, and one copper bead.

7 Repeat the first half of Step 5 after stringing all the beads. Set aside.

8 Next you'll create the chain that attaches to either end of the beaded strand. Cut eight 1½" (3.8 cm) pieces of 16-gauge copper wire. File ends smooth. Use round-nose pliers to bend each end of the short wire pieces in toward the center making a figure eight. Repeat for all eight pieces of wire.

fig. **1**

fig. **2**

fig. **3**

fig. **4**

WHAT WORKS FOR YOUR CORE WIRE?

Really, any wire will do. Usually I find myself going for sterling wire as the core wire because I like the shiny wire that peeks out between the spreading coil. However, with the cost of silver reaching a record high, it seems a waste to hide it. So, reach for copper or brass or steel instead.

9   With two chain-nose pliers, hold either side of the figure eight and turn one side a half turn. Repeat for all eight short pieces of wire.

10   Open one of the loops of a figure-eight link as you would a jump ring. Attach it to another link, and close the loop. Open the free loop on the new link and attach a third link. Continue until you have four links connected together. Repeat to make a second four-link chain. Set aside.

11   The clasp shown is a variation on the simple S-clasp (shown on page 21). Use round-nose pliers to form a small loop at one end of a 4" (10 cm) piece of 16-gauge copper wire. With a 15" (38 cm) piece of 22-gauge sterling silver wire, coil a 2" (5 cm) area of the 16-gauge wire. Trim the excess wire from the end of the coil closest to the starting loop. Push the coil so that it is close to the starting loop. Leave the excess wire at the other end.

12   Insert the tip of your round-nose pliers back inside the starting loop of the clasp. Turn the loop in toward the coil-covered wire forming a larger loop. Continue turning the wire in until the coiled areas overlap. With the excess sterling wire, wrap over top of the precious coil. Trim excess and file smooth.

13   Use round-nose pliers to create the hook portion of the clasp. Trim excess wire about ⅛" (3 mm) longer than needed. Form a small loop in the end of the wire to match the beginning loop. (**Figure 4**)

14   Oxidize the two pieces of chain and the clasp in liver of sulfur (see page 26), and then use extrafine steel wool to polish back the oxidation. Tumble the chain for about 20 minutes in a rotary tumbler.

15   Attach a length of chain to each end of the beaded strand by opening the last link on each chain with chain-nose pliers. Close the loop.

16   Open the last link of the figure-eight chain and attach it to the clasp. Close the loop.

TECHNIQUES

Coiling

Patina

Chunky wrapped loops

Simple loops

Jump rings

TOOLS

Round-nose pliers

Chain-nose pliers

Wire cutters

Punch pliers

¼" (6 mm) mandrel

⅛" (3 mm) mandrel

Alphabet stamps

Utility hammer

Ammonia

Salt water

Spritz bottle

Sealant

Paintbrush

Polishing cloth

MATERIALS

8' (2.4 m) 18-gauge brass wire

3' (91.5 cm) 20-gauge brass wire

4' (1.2 m) 20-gauge colored copper wire (color shown: antique bronze)

15' (4.5 m) 24-gauge colored copper (color shown: blue)

Fourteen ½" x ¾" (1.3 cm x 2 cm) brass drop blanks

36" (91 cm) length of brass chain

Three 8mm lampwork-glass striped beads

Lampwork beads by Kerry Bogert

Finshed size: 26" (66 cm) lariat

wash away
LARIAT

Too few people truly appreciate a rainy day. It brings the opportunity to make an extra cup of tea, grab a book, and curl up under a blanket near a toasty fire. Bring on the rain, I say! And for the days when the sun beats down and I am wishing I could wash it away, I have my own wire raindrops in this lariat-style necklace.

fig. 1

fig. 2

fig. 3

1. For this project, start by pre-oxidizing the brass wire that will be used. Loosely wind 8' (244 cm) of 18-gauge brass wire. Use the ammonia oxidizing technique (shown on page 27) to blacken the wire. Once darkened, remove the wire from the ammonia fumes and set aside.

2. Next, using the salt water patina technique (shown on page 28), you will patina the brass drops. Place six brass drops in the ammonia container floating them above the liquid and before sealing it, spritz the pieces with salt water. Once you have reached the level of blue you are looking for, remove the brass drops from the container and allow to air-dry.

3. While the patina is forming on the blank brass drops, use alphabet stamps and your bench block to stamp the letters W A S H A W A Y, one letter each, on the eight remaining brass drops (**Figure 1**). Once the blue patina drops have been removed from the ammonia fumes, place these stamped drops in the same container. Do not spray these with salt water. Remove when they start to darken slightly.

TIP: There will be some residual salt water on the platform you place these stamped drops on. So, they will pick up random hints of blue without completely changing.

4. When the blue patina brass drops have dried, seal the finish with sealant using a paintbrush. Coat one side at a time allowing the sealer to dry before coating the opposite side.

5. With punch pliers, add a hole to each brass drop. Set aside. (**Figure 2**)

6. From the brass wire oxidized in Step 1, cut eight 3" (7.5 cm) pieces from the 18-gauge wire with wire cutters.

7. Using the blue, antique bronze, and brass wire, coil a 1½" (3.8 cm) area of each piece of the 18-gauge wire. Make four blue, two antique bronze, and two brass. Trim excess wire and file smooth. (**Figure 3**)

8   Situate the coil on the 18-gauge wire so that it is about 1″ (2.5 cm) from one end. Repeat for the other seven coils. Wrap the coil-covered wire around the ¼″ (6 mm) mandrel just once. Bring the ends of the coiled area together, and wrap the 18-gauge core wire twice with the longer exposed end of wire (**Figure 4**). Trim excess wrapped wire. Set aside and repeat with the other seven coil-covered pieces.

9   With round-nose pliers, form a simple loop with the remaining wire that extends past the coiled area (**Figure 5**). Repeat for the other wire raindrops.

10 Use a polishing cloth to rub back the oxidation on the simple loops of each wire raindrop. Set aside.

11 Use a 2′ (61 cm) piece of pre-oxidized 18-gauge brass wire to coil around a ⅛″ (3 mm) mandrel. Use this coil to create fourteen jump rings. Attach the jump rings to the fourteen brass drops. Set aside.

12 With the remaining pre-oxidized brass wire, form three individual chunky wrapped loop links with the three striped lampwork beads. Set aside.

13 Cut from your length of chain a 2½″ (6.5 cm) piece. Open the last link in the chain and attach it to one of the beaded links. Open the simple loops of the wire drops and link them to the piece of chain. Open the jump rings of the A W A Y stamped drops and add them to the chain as well. Between the wire drops and the brass letter drops, open the jump rings on three of the patinaed brass drops and attach them to the chain. (**Figure 6**)

fig. **4**

fig. **5**

fig. **6**

fig. **7**

14 Cut from the length of chain a ½" (1.3 cm) piece. Open the last link in the chain and attach it to the free loop on the beaded link used in Step 13. Open the last link at the opposite end of the chain piece and attach it to one of the loops of another beaded link. (**Figure 7**)

15 Open the first link of a 2' (61 cm) length of chain. Attach the chain to the free loop of the beaded link used in Step 14. About 6" (15 cm) from the free end of the chain, open a link and connect both the chain pieces to either end of the third beaded link.

16 Open the simple loops of the wire drops and link them to the end of the chain after the third beaded link. Open the jump rings of the W A S H stamped drops and add them to the chain as well. Between the wire drops and the brass letter drops, open the jump rings on three of the patinaed brass drops and attach them to the chain.

alternate view

Not a fan of lariats? Try this design! All the components are created using the same methods described, but the pieces are attached to the center of the chain, and copper was used in place of brass. Heat patina was used on the copper teardrops, stamped with the words L O V E L Y D A Y. Add a beautifully enameled toggle clasp by ckoopbeads.com to enhance the color palette.

WASH AWAY LARIAT •

TECHNIQUES

Wrapped loops

Ear wire

Patina

TOOLS

Round-nose pliers

Chain-nose pliers

Wire cutters

Liver of sulfur

Polishing cloth

MATERIALS

18" (45.5 cm) 16-gauge copper wire

6" (15 cm) 20-gauge sterling silver wire

Two 15mm lampwork-glass straight-sided lentils

Lampwork beads by Claudia Pagel

Finished size: 2½" (6.5 cm)

just because
EARRINGS

When asked why the beads in your earrings don't match, answer 'just because.' Because you wonder who said earrings have to match. Because you are only as old as you feel and are even younger at heart. Because anything is possible. Because stripes and swirls go together like peanut butter and jelly. Because there is the distance of a huge smile between each ear. And because you can.

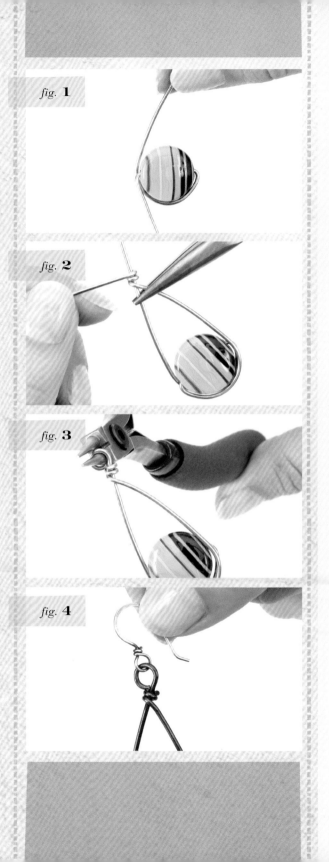

fig. **1**

fig. **2**

fig. **3**

fig. **4**

1 You are going to be pleasantly surprised just how quickly these earrings are wired up. Begin by cutting two pieces of 16-gauge copper wire to 9" (23 cm) lengths.

2 Slide one of the lampwork beads onto the center of the 9" (23 cm) piece of copper wire. Wrap the wire around one side of the bead following its contours (**Figure 1**). Do this with both sides of the wire so that they end up running side by side along what will be the bottom half of the bead.

3 Bring the wire ends together about 1" (2.5 cm) from the top of the bead. Hold the wires in place with your chain-nose pliers and wrap one wire around the other as you would to close a wrapped loop (**Figure 2**). Trim the excess wrapped wire.

4 Trim the remaining length of wire to about ⅝" (1.5 cm) and use round-nose pliers to form a simple loop. (**Figure 3**)

5 Repeat Steps 2–4 for the second earring.

6 Place the earring components in a liver of sulfur solution until the copper blackens (see page 26). This should take less than 1 minute.

7 Remove the components from the LOS and very lightly polish. Do not overpolish the wire and reveal the red color. Light polishing will give the copper a gunmetal coloring.

8 Dangle from your favorite style ear wires constructed from the 20-gauge sterling silver wire. (**Figure 4**)

REMEMBER OXIDATION RATES

When mixing metals, as we have here, it is important to keep in mind that some metals oxidize faster than others. For example, copper oxidizes in a matter of seconds when in liver of sulfur compared to sterling silver, which needs several minutes to start to darken. It is best to oxidize the components individually to achieve a more uniform level of patina.

TECHNIQUES

Wrapped loops

Chunky wrapped loops

Coiling

Clasps

TOOLS

Round-nose pliers

Chain-nose pliers

Wire cutters

Coiling Gizmo

MATERIALS

4" (10 cm) 16-gauge copper wire

3.5' (106 cm) 18-gauge colored copper wire (color shown: vintage bronze)

12' (3.6 m) 20-gauge colored copper wire (color shown: vintage bronze)

Five enameled metal rings in graduated sizes ⅜–1" (1–2.5 cm)

Twelve turquoise size 8° glass seed beads

Twenty-four white-lined amber size 11° glass seed beads

15" (38 cm) length of brass chain

One 3" (7.5 cm) lampwork-glass focal disc

Lampwork beads by Kerry Bogert

Finished size: 20" (51 cm)

the mariner NECKLACE

The sea holds such a myriad of treasures. Some are natural, such as brilliantly colored reef fish and shapely shells. Some are man-made, such as sunken ships and mermaid tales. In his net, the mariner finds all manner of special trinkets. Perhaps this large glass disc was one of them. In it is captured the echo of waves, the warmth of a sunset, and it calls to return to the sea.

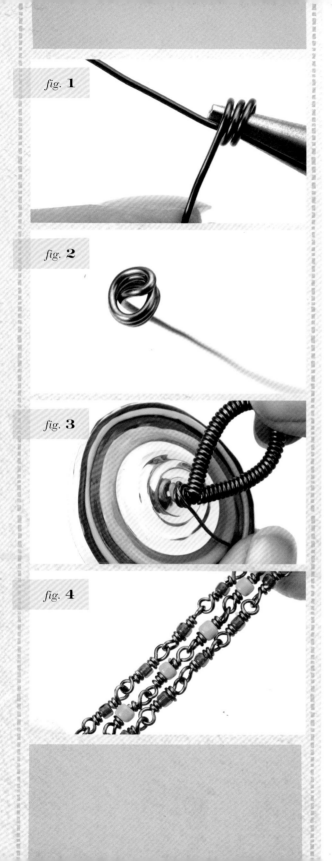

fig. 1

fig. 2

fig. 3

fig. 4

1   With round-nose pliers in hand, this design begins with creating the bail for the pendant. Using an 8″ (20.5 cm) piece of 20-gauge wire, loosely wrap the pliers' jaws four times (**Figure 1**). This creates a wire-style French knot. Slide the lampwork disc bead onto the wire knot and set aside.

2   Using a Coiling Gizmo, create a 2¾″ (7 cm) coil from 20-gauge colored copper wire. Trim excess wire and remove from the gizmo.

3   Slide the coil piece onto the wire protruding from the back side of the lampwork focal bead. Form a loop in the coil and with the remaining 20-gauge colored copper wire, wrap the coil loop closed as you would a chunky wrapped loop (**Figure 2**). Trim excess wire. Bend the coiled loop so that it lies against the back of the lampwork disc. This is now the bail of your pendant. Set aside.

4   Using the linking wrapped loop technique (shown on page 15), create three 5″ (12.5 cm) lengths of chain out of the seed beads. One length will use the turquoise seed beads, and two will use the white core amber seed beads. (**Figure 3**)

CARING FOR GLASS BEADS

Lampwork glass is very durable but not indestructible. When working with lampwork, remember that you are working with a miniature work of art and treat it as such. Glass doesn't like to be dropped on concrete or abandoned in the bottom of your gym bag. Treat the beads with respect, and they will last for generations.

THE MARINER NECKLACE •

5 Begin another wrapped loop and before closing the loop, connect to the ends of the three beaded chains from Step 4. Make a second wrapped loop on the other end of the same piece of wire and connect it to the pendant bail. When wrapping the loop closed, wrap it over the top of the previous wrappings in the chunky-loop style. (**Figure 5**)

6 At the other end of the three beaded strands, again connect them with a wrapped loop. Form a second wrapped loop that connects to a small enameled ring and finish the wrapping in the chunky technique. Set aside.

7 Arrange the four remaining enameled metal rings in order from largest to smallest. Connect each one to the next with the chunky-style wrapped-loop links described in Steps 5 and 6.

8 Then, connect the largest enameled ring to the pendant bail and add another chunky wrapped link to the smaller link. This does not connect to anything, but it will act as the catch for your clasp. (**Figure 6**)

9 Cut to length two 7¼" (18.5 cm) lengths of brass chain. Set aside.

10 Create a wrapped loop link with a single turquoise seed bead that connects to the single enameled ring on the chain side of the design. When wrapping the loop closed on the opposite side of the seed bead, connect it to the last two links in each of the two pieces of brass chain. (**Figure 7**)

11 Using 16-gauge copper wire, make an S-clasp that starts with a closed spiral. Lightly oxidize the clasp. Then, attach it to the two lengths of brass chain. Rather than joining at the back of the neck, this clasp sets off to the lower right front side of the neck. (**Figure 8**)

fig. **5**

fig. **6**

fig. **7**

fig. **8**

TECHNIQUES

Simple loops

Wrapped loops

Coiling

Patina

Clasps

TOOLS

Round-nose pliers

Chain-nose pliers

Wire cutters

¼" (6 mm) steel mandrel

Ammonia

Resealable container

MATERIALS

3" (7.5 cm) 16-gauge brass wire

6' (1.8 m) 18-gauge brass wire

6" (15 cm) 20-gauge brass wire

7 lampwork-glass head pins

Lampwork beads by Kerry Bogert

Finshed size: 7½" (19 cm)

modern plaiting
BRACELET

When I was a little girl, I had long straight hair that
was almost always set in two braids. As an adult, I still
love to braid my hair, but for those days when I can't,
I have this sweet bracelet to don. Brass wire has been
woven into a plait with playful mod-style dotted beads.
The juxtaposition of the warm oxidized brass against
the clustered cool-tone dangles is both refreshing and
wearable.

1 The braid of wire is the main focus of this bracelet and the part you'll begin with. Cut three pieces of 18-gauge brass wire to 24" (61 cm) lengths.

2 Bend the three pieces of wire in half around the ¼" (6 mm) steel mandrel. Use the chain-nose pliers to bring the path of the wires close together and taut around the mandrel.

3 Tightly coil a 6" (15 cm) piece of 20-gauge brass wire around the wires, securing them all together. Trim excess 20-gauge wire. (**Figure 1**)

4 Divide the six lengths of wire into three sections, each with two wires.

5 Braid the wire: Cross the leftmost section of wire over the center, so it is now the center. (What was the center will now be the left.) Cross the right section of wire over the center, making it the new center section (with what was the center now pushed to the right). Again, cross the left section to the center, and then the right.

6 Continue braiding the wire in this fashion until you have 6" (15 cm) of braided wire.

7 Take the leftmost section of wire and wrap it around the two other sections. Take one of the two wire pieces from that first section and wrap it half a wrap farther than the other, so that now there is a tail of wire splayed out on either side of the wrapped area (**Figure 2**). Trim each tail of wire to ⅜" (1 cm) and use round-nose pliers to form a simple loop. Remove the mandrel at this time.

TIP: I keep the mandrel in until this point because it makes holding the wire while braiding a lot easier.

8 Bend three of the center pieces of wire back toward the braid of wire. Trim each to ⅜" (1 cm) and form a simple loop. You should now have five simple loops at the end of the braid of wire and one center piece of wire remaining. (**Figure 3**)

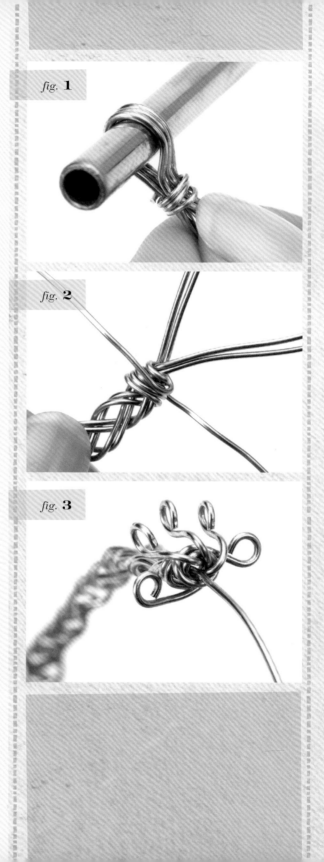

fig. **1**

fig. **2**

fig. **3**

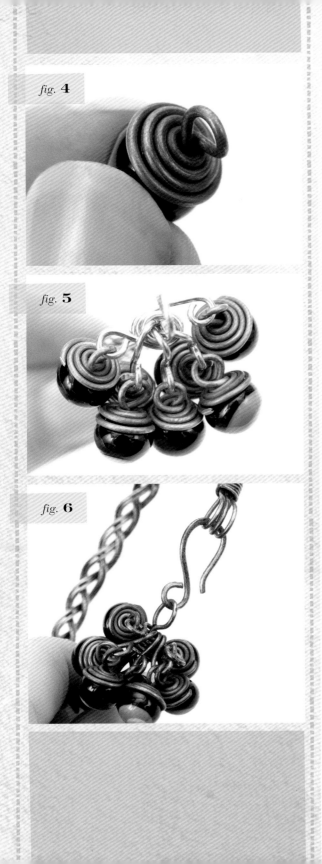

fig. 4

fig. 5

fig. 6

9 Trim the center piece of wire to ½" (1.3 cm) and form a simple loop with round-nose pliers. This loop will be slightly larger than the previous five. Set aside.

10 Form the straight end of a glass head pin into a wrapped loop. Keep the loop tight against the head of the pin and wrap the tail of wire into a spiral around the center loop (**Figure 4**). Repeat this on all head pins for a total of seven.

11 With chain-nose pliers, open the first simple loop in the series of five loops on the braided portion of the bracelet. Add one dangle and close the loop. Repeat this adding two dangles to the second loop, one dangle to the third loop, two dangles to the fourth loop, and one dangle to the fifth loop. Set aside. (**Figure 5**)

12 Make a simple S-clasp as shown on page 21 and attach it to the larger tool near the dangle cluster on the bracelet. The starting loop of wires acts as the catch for your clasp. (**Figure 6**)

13 Wrap the braid of wire around a bracelet mandrel to form it to the shape of your wrist. You may want to set the mandrel aside after the initial shaping and mold the bracelet by hand to a nice oval shape.

14 Using the patina process explained on page 27, oxidize the brass wire with ammonia in a resealable bag.

15 Once the wire darkens, remove it from the container and polish back the oxidation.

TECHNIQUES

Wrapped loops

Spiraling

Hammering

Patina

TOOLS

Round-nose pliers

Chain-nose pliers

Wire cutters

Chasing hammer

Bench block

Liver of sulfur

Polishing cloth

Craft mat

Alcohol inks (colors shown: currant, cranberry, eggplant, wild plum)

Sealant

Fray Stop

MATERIALS

6" (15 cm) 16-gauge copper wire

7.5' (2.3 m) 18-gauge copper wire

36" (91.5 cm) length of 4mm wide silk ribbon

Three 12mm lampwork-glass round beads

8mm large-hole rondelle spacer beads

Lampwork beads by Kerry Bogert

Finshed size: 7½" (19 cm)

western ways BRACELET

There is something about this bracelet that makes me want to buy a vintage pair of cowgirl boots and spend an evening dancing at a barn party. Maybe it is the soft texture of the silk ribbon or the wispy webs of purple glass trailing to the edges of these beads. Regardless, it is sure to add a swirled-up bit of spunk to your soul.

fig. 1

fig. 2

fig. 3

1 This bracelet comes together quickly once you have made the spiraled wire dangles, so we'll start there. Cut fifteen pieces of 18-gauge wire to random lengths of 4–6″ (10–15 cm).

2 With round-nose pliers, make a wrapped loop at one end of a single piece of 18-gauge wire. Trim excess wire. Then, make a closed spiral (shown on page 16) with the tail of wire. (**Figure 1**)

3 Using the chasing hammer and bench block, flatten then tool the surface of the wire spiral. (**Figure 2**)

4 Repeat Steps 2 and 3 for the remaining fourteen pieces of wire. Set aside.

5 Make an S-shaped clasp. Also make a figure-eight link to act as the catch for the clasp. Flatten and texture the arches of the clasp and the loops of the figure eight as you did the dangles.

6 Lightly oxidize the dangles and clasp components in liver of sulfur. Buff back the oxidation to highlight texture.

7 Lay out the dangles on a craft mat and apply droplets of colored alcohol inks to the tooled surface of the spirals (see page 31). Allow to dry. (**Figure 3**)

8 Once the patina is completely dry, seal with sealant. (Patina has not been applied to the clasp components, so it is not necessary to seal them.)

9 String a piece of silk cording through the closed loop of your S-clasp. Bring both ends of the silk ribbon together so that it is half its original length.

10 Tie a knot using both strands of the silk ribbon tight against the clasp.

11 You should now have two strands of ribbon coming off the end of the clasp. On one of the strands, string one spacer bead, tie a knot, one lampwork bead, tie a knot, and string another spacer bead (**Figure 4**). On the opposite strand, string five spiral wire dangles. Then, tie a knot with both strands of silk together (**Figure 5**).

12 Repeat Step 11 two more times.

13 After the final knot, string another spacer bead that goes on both strands of silk ribbon. String on the figure-eight portion of the clasp. Then pass both ends of the silk ribbon back through the spacer bead. (**Figure 6**)

14 Tie another knot with both strands of silk ribbon. Trim excess ribbon to 2″ (5 cm) and treat the ends of the silk ribbon with Fray Stop.

fig. **4**

fig. **5**

fig. **6**

ADJUSTABLE JEWELRY

For jewelry designers who sell their work, be it online or at art shows, knowing how to size bracelets so they fit a variety of possible buyers can be a challenge. Bracelets like this are great because they are easily adjusted to different sizes without having to completely remake the piece. Simple loosen the final knot and pull out the loop where the figure-eight portion of the clasp is, then tighten the knot. This makes it almost effortless to add an extra ½″ (1.3 cm) or so.

MEET THE BEAD ARTISTS

Behind every great jewelry design are beautifully crafted beads. Glass beads, in particular, hold a special place in my heart, as do the lampwork artists pouring their passion into each little creation they make. The projects in this book would not have been possible without the amazing inspiration found in the unique beads I had the pleasure of working with. An extra-special thanks goes to these incredible artists.

Mika Collins is a Japanese woman living in beautiful Skagit Valley, Washington, with her husband and two amazing boys. She has been making lampwork beads for about eight years. She loves to watch glass melt and see simple glass rods become beautiful and intricate beads. You can find her beadwork at pinocean.etsy.com.

J. C. Herrell was working as a corporate trainer when she began to teach herself lampworking in 2001. She has a fondness for working with enamels but has a strong desire to control stringers and create designs with fine, straight lines inspired by a long history of architectural interest, too. J. C. currently works from a home studio on the coast of California exploring color and line as a means of expression on the canvas of a glass bead. Visit jcherrell.com to learn more.

Yee Kwan is irresistibly drawn to bright and colorful things. It's no wonder that she loves to work with glass! Yee is happiest when doing something with her hands—be it lampworking, sewing, knitting, or silversmithing. A Canadian transplanted to the South, she is currently attending grad school for nurse anesthesia and is blessed to have her best friend as her husband. Yee's motto carpe diem, or "seize the day," is evident in the varied designs and styles that often find their way into her work, which can be found at theglassturtle.etsy.com.

Anne Lichtenstein is a mom, artist, and serial crafter living in Upstate New York with her husband and teenage daughter. Six years ago her daughter's art teacher introduced her to the craft of making glass beads; she has been hypnotized by the flame ever since. She now works out of her own studio making glass beads, which has grown to include work with enamel and mixed metals. You can find Anne's glass beads and other jewelry components in her Etsy shop, gardannebeads.etsy.com.

Claudia Pagel worked for ten years as a graphic designer in Paris after attending a fine arts school in Germany. She discovered glass beads quite by accident while searching for mosaic supplies. Working on a torch lent to her by her husband, she started teaching herself to make lampwork beads, later taking workshops with world-renowned glass instructors. You can view more of Claudia's work at glasting.com.

Melissa Rediger, a kindergarten teacher, is also a mother to four young children. She lives in a small town in Iowa and when not making beads, she enjoys incorporating her beads into jewelry and working on her website, mjrbeads.com.

Ali VandeGrift is a scientific glassblower and glass beadmaker living in Tennessee, working at Oak Ridge National Laboratory. She has been working with glass since the age of fifteen and hopes to live a life fully immersed in the medium. While glass takes up most of her time, she also enjoys kayaking, gardening, and chasing her two small dogs. Check out her available work at aliveglass.etsy.com.

Aja Vaz has been a lampwork artist since late 2005, mostly self-taught and in love with organic styles. Currently perched in North Carolina, she lives an adventurous life married to a military man and chasing after her young son. She has been published in *Bead Review 3* and keeps a blog (wanderingspirit-designs.blogspot.com) where she shows her work before listing it on Etsy.

Kelley Wenzel likes to play with fire and run with scissors, but not at the same time. She loves kissing her kids, watching her husband smile, and photographing all those wonderful moments in between. Find her lampwork beads at kelleysbeads.etsy.com.

Yours truly . . . Yes, I, *Kerry Bogert*, your ever-faithful author and jewelry designer, am a lampwork-glass artist, too. I began making beads in 2005 after drooling over artist Cassie Donlen's lampwork. If beads could be made by hand, and look that cool, I knew I had to learn to do it! I have had a love affair with glass and color ever since. You can find my beads at kabsconcepts.com.

RESOURCES

My favorite places to find all the whatnots a jeweler needs . . .

The Beadin' Path
(207) 865-4785
beadinpath.com

Beaducation
(650) 261-1870
beaducation.com

Blue Buddha Boutique
(866) 602-7464
bluebuddhaboutique.com

C-Koop Beads
2159 Shilhon Rd.
Duluth, MN 55804
(218) 525-7333
ckoopbeads.com

Fire Mountain Gems
(800) 423-2319
firemountaingems.com

Fundametals
fundametals.net

Jewelry Supply
(916) 780-9610
jewelrysupply.com

Lowe's Home Improvement
lowes.com

Objects and Elements
(206) 965-0373
objectsandelements.com

Out on a Whim
(800) 232-3111
whimbeads.com

Painting with Fire Artwear
paintingwithfireartwear.com

Paramount Wire Co.
(973) 672-0500
parawire.com

Ranger Ink
(732) 389-3535
rangerink.com

ReHouse Architectural Salvage
rehouse.com

Rio Grande
(800) 545-6566
riogrande.com

Sculpt Nouveau
(800) 728-5787
sculptnouveau.com

Tickle Me Beads
ticklemebeads.com

Thunderbird Supply
(800) 545-7968
thunderbirdsupply.com

Vintaj Natural Brass Company
vintaj.com

individual project items

AMONG ANEMONE
steel wire: Lowe's Home Improvement; *sterling silver wire:* Rio Grande; *beads:* Yee Kwan theglassturtle.etsy.com

ANALOG
steel wire: Lowe's Home Improvement; *colored wire:* Parawire; *beads:* Mika Collins pinocean.etsy.com

AURORA
copper wire and sheet metal: Rio Grande; *rolo chain:* Vintaj; *beads:* Kerry Bogert kabsconcepts.com

BLOOMING TWINE
brass wire: Rio Grande; *brass blanks:* Vintaj; *beads:* Kerry Bogert kabsconcepts.com

CANDY CHANDELIERS
steel wire: Lowe's Home Improvement; *sterling silver wire:* Rio Grande; *beads:* Kerry Bogert kabsconcepts.com

CHRYSANTHEMUM
steel metal: Rio Grande; *colored wire:* Parawire; *chain:* Vintaj; *beads:* Kerry Bogert kabsconcepts.com

CREEK HILL
chain: Vintaj; *beads:* Mika Collins pinocean.etsy.com

HIDDEN GRACE
brass sheet metal and wire: Rio Grande; *silk ribbon:* local bead store; *lampwork cabochon:* Kerry Bogert kabsconcepts.com

JUST BECAUSE
copper and sterling silver wire: Rio Grande; *beads:* Claudia Pagel glasting.com

LAZY DAISY
blank brass disc: Vintaj; *chain:* doubleangeldesign.etsy.com; *colored wire:* Parawire; *beads:* Kerry Bogert kabsconcepts.com

LILACS AND PEONIES
sterling silver: Rio Grande; *beads:* Kerry Bogert kabsconcepts.com

LUNA UNEARTHED
steel wire: Lowe's Home Improvement; *sterling silver:* Rio Grande; *beads:* Kerry Bogert kabsconcepts.com

THE MARINER
seed beads: Out on a Whim; *chain:* doubleangeldesign.etsy.com; *enamel rings:* Fundametals; *colored wire:* Parawire; *beads:* Kerry Bogert kabsconcepts.com

MODERN PLAITING
brass wire: Rio Grande; *lampwork head pins:* Kerry Bogert kabsconcepts.com

MOROCCAN ARCHWAYS
copper wire: Rio Grande; *chain:* doubleangeldesign.etsy.com; *seed beads:* Out on a Whim; *beads:* Aja Vaz wanderingspirit.etsy.com

MOUNTAIN BRIDE
brass wire: Rio Grande; *alcohol inks:* Ranger; *beads:* Anne Lichtenstein gardannebeads.etsy.com

SAFE PASSAGE
brass wire: Rio Grande; *lock plate:* ReHouse; *sari cording:* Objects and Elements; *beads:* Melissa Rediger mjrbeads.com

SEAHORSE TALES
brass wire: Rio Grande; *curb chain:* Vintaj; *beads:* Ali VandeGrift alivebeads.etsy.com

SPICE TRADERS
ornate brass discs: Vintaj; *alcohol inks:* Ranger; *colored copper wire:* Parawire; *sterling silver wire and sheet metal brass:* Rio Grande; *seed beads:* Out on a Whim

SPROCKETS IN POCKETS
copper and sterling silver wire: Rio Grande; *beads:* J. C. Herrell jcherrell .com

SWIFTLY BOUND
colored wires: Parawire; *beading wire and crimps:* Fire Mountain Gems; *copper beads:* Painting with Fire Artwear; *beads:* Kerry Bogert kabsconcepts.com

TENDER NEST
brass wire: Rio Grande; *blank brass discs:* Vintaj; *silk cording:* Painting with Fire Artwear; *beads:* Kelley Wenzel kelleysbeads.etsy.com

WASH AWAY
chain: doubleangeldesign.etsy.com; *brass drops:* Fundametals; *colored wire:* Parawire; *beads:* Kerry Bogert kabsconcepts.com

WESTERN WAYS
silk ribbon and spacer beads: local bead store; *copper wire:* Rio Grande; *beads:* Kerry Bogert kabsconcepts .com

WONDER WHILE YOU WANDER
sterling strip and wire: Rio Grande; *colored wire:* Parawire; *beads:* Kerry Bogert kabsconcepts.com

INDEX

alcohol ink patina 31
ammonia and salt water patina 28–29, 31

backstitch 34
bench block 6
bench pin 8, 9
big "daddy" cutters 6
blanket stitch 35
brass 13
brass patina 27–30, 31

chain-nose pliers 6, 7
chain stitch 35
chunky wrapped loops 15
clasps 21–23
cloth, polishing 7
coiling 19–20
coiling tool 7
cold connections 9
color 36–37
copper 12, 13
copper patina 26, 27–30, 31
craft sealers 32
cutters, 6, 8, 9

dapping tools 8, 9
disc cutter 8, 9
drawing a bead 19

ear wires 23–25
embroidery, wire 33–35

files 7
findings, making 20–25
fire brick 9
fishhook ear wires 23–24
flush cutters 6, 7
French ear wires 24–25

gauge 10, 11
glass beads care 117

hammer, chasing 7; texture 8
head pins 17–18
heat patina 27–28, 31
hook clasp 21–22
hoop ear wires 25

jeweler's saw 8, 9
jump rings 20

liver of sulfur (LOS) 26–27, 31
loops, chunky wrapped 15; simple 16; wrapped 14

mallet, nylon 6
mandrels 7
metal preparation for patina 26
metal snips 8, 9
micro torch 8, 9

patina, oxidized 26–27
pliers 6, 7, 8
potato chip patina 30, 31
punch pliers 8
punches, replacement 8

rosary pliers see round-nose pliers
rotary tool 8
round-nose pliers 6, 7
running stitch 34
rusting metal 32

saw, jeweler's 8, 9
S-clasp 21

sealants 32
sheet metal 10
simple loops 16
spirals 16–17
spray sealers, aerosol 32
stainless steel shot 7
stamps, alphabet 8, 9
steel 13; rusting 32
steel wool 7
sterling silver 12
sterling silver patina 26, 31
stitches, wire embroidery 34–35

toggle clasp 22–23
tumbler 7

vinegar patina 29, 31

wax sealant 32
whipstitch 35
wire 10–13
wire hardness 11
work-hardening 11
wrapped-loop links 15
wrapped loops 14–16

TWIST, WRAP, AND SET YOUR WAY TO LOVELY JEWELRY

with these inspired resources from Interweave